STREET SURVIVAL SKILLS

MIKE McBRIDE

GW00770986

First edition November 1996

ISBN 0 85164 076 1

Police Review
Publishing Co Ltd
100 Avenue Road
London NW3 3PG

Designed and Typeset by
Hairy Toffee Graphic Design Service
London SW12 8JF
Photographs by Grant Ardern and M J McBride
Origination by AJD Imaging
London E14 9RL
Printed by The Alden Press
Osney Mead, Oxford

ACKNOWLEDGEMENTS

I would like to thank, Chief Constable J Mervyn Jones QPM MSc (Cheshire Constabulary) and Superintendent GE Gerrard BA, for giving me their permission to write the book.

I also acknowledge the support of Mr FHJ Broughton (Chairman of the Police Federation of England and Wales) who has approved the contents of this book.

This alphabetical list gives credit to those people whose encouragement and support helped me to produce this work.

Mr W Andrew (FBI), Mr E Bauer (Civil Defence Supply), Inspector P Boatman (Northamptonshire), Captain G Brennan (Los Angeles Police Department), Ex-Chief Superintendent KJ Croasdell, Sergeant C Clarke (Cheshire), Inspector J Davison (Metropolitan), Ms M Dawkins (PRG), Mr D Elam (Quik-Kuf), Constable S Fraser (Derbyshire), Mr J Gillings (Cheshire), Superintendent B Gresty (Merseyside), Constable M Greville (Strathclyde), Inspector CR Howarth (Cheshire), Sergeant L Kerr (Training Support, Harrogate), Inspector S Kissane (Hertfordshire), Inspector G Lawrence (West Midlands), Inspector M Laux MA BSc (Hampshire), Constable D Peebles (Lancashire), Ms S Phillips BA (University of Birmingham), Mrs C Rimmer (Professional Development Officer), Inspector C Richards BA (Cheshire), Mr T Sheldon (PSDB), Inspector J Smith (Cheshire), Mr T Smith (Monadnock), Sergeant M Tasker (Cheshire), Detective Constable M Toker QPM (Cheshire), Sergeant R White (Cheshire), Chief Inspector D Williams (Kent), Ms C Wilson PhD (National Police Research Unit - Australia), Constable N Woodward (Cheshire).

Most of the photographs were taken by Sergeant RG Ardern (Cheshire) and processed by the Cheshire Constabulary Photographic Section, Mr R Biddle.

Last, but by no means least, I owe my wife (Elaine) and my daughter (Fiona) special thanks for putting up with me.

DISCLAIMER

The Police Federation of England and Wales supports officer safety and has provided a foreword to this book.

The aim of the book is to assist the operational police officer to improve his or her safety and every effort has been made to ensure its accuracy. The author, publisher and the Police Federation of England and Wales shall not accept liability for errors or omissions or any loss or damage caused due to the information contained in this book.

Ultimately, each officer has to justify his or her own actions based on the circumstances at the time.

FOREWORD

When I first achieved a position of influence within the Police Federation, the first thing I did was to initiate an officer safety programme. My own experience of training and equipment was one of disbelief. For our police service not to train and equip officers for the 1990s was beyond belief. Things changed, not only because of the Police Federation, but because 34 police officers were murdered and over 300,000 were assaulted since 1980.

This book reflects and consolidates so much of the good practice and will become an essential aid to those who consider officer safety. The most important aspect of training is that the operational officer understands, can use, and relates to the advice that is offered. This book does all those things, it is not just a trainers manual. It will become a book that makes a difference. The prize is an effective, traditional, unarmed British Police Service. Well worth striving for.

F H J Broughton

Chairman

Police Federation of England & Wales

PREFACE

In the police radio room, it was turning out to be just another ordinary shift. Out on the street, a young police officer was just pulling a van over for a routine check. No-one had any idea that a few seconds later, the radio would crackle with the emergency call that the officer had received multiple gunshot wounds.

The officer was on solo patrol in a marked police car. He stopped the van to speak to the occupants. After obtaining the personal details of the driver and front seat passenger the officer went to speak to the man in the back. The officer found himself looking at an automatic pistol. Instantly, the officer had turned and was running for cover. There were five shots. He was hit three times in the stomach and legs and was left for dead in the road, as the van sped off. Only through luck, medical expertise and the sheer will to live, did he survive.

This was not South Central Los Angeles or Washington DC, nor a lawless suburb of Moscow, this was Warrington, Cheshire on a Thursday night.

In our work, we may encounter firearms and edged weapons anywhere and in any situation. Whether you patrol in a metropolitan area, or the quietest of rural districts, you face the potential risk of injury or death. Have you ever thought how you would deal with a life-threatening situation?

By developing street survival skills, you will become more confident in handling incidents and be able to act without hesitation to protect both yourself and the public.

CONTENTS

Chapter one

INTRODUCTION

Keypoints

Use this chapter to find out:

I *Why the image of the police officer has changed.*

I *What are the Street Survival Skills.*

Chapter one

Introduction

Policing Britain's streets today has probably never been more difficult for operational police officers, who face increased threats of assault and injury whilst performing their job; and at the same time, their actions are subjected to greater and greater scrutiny, for example by town centre CCTV cameras and even bystanders with camcorders.

Other workers are injured or killed in the course of their work, but what makes the experience of being a police officer unique is that people assault officers because of what they represent. There is a malicious intent in many of the attacks upon the police. Whilst readers cannot change this fact, they must not accept that being assaulted is all part of the job.

This book is designed to give operational police officers an informative assessment of the risks they face on patrol. Skills and routine procedures will be explained which are intended to minimise those risks. The responsibility for officer safety starts with each individual officer and developing Street Survival Skills is the first step.

The chances of a police officer being assaulted are three times greater than that of an ordinary member of the public; the risks increase dramatically for those officers engaged in operational duties. By its nature police work is dangerous and there is a widespread belief among officers that the risks of being assaulted are increasing. There is, however, an even greater risk of serious injury or death by involvement in a road traffic accident, this book provides guidance on police driving to reduce this risk.

ALTERED IMAGE

Over the past few years, the traditional image of the British police officer has changed radically. The sight of patrolling officers in body armour with rigid handcuffs and batons is no longer uncommon on Britain's streets.

Why has this change come about? It is not necessarily due to any significant increase in assaults. (National statistics have only been published for a comparatively short period of time, and do not bear out any real trend one way or another.)

Chief officers have decided to provide protective equipment and training for a variety of reasons:

I The prospect of civil actions from officers unprepared or ill-equipped to deal with confrontational situations.

I Health and safety legislation.

The changing image of the British police officer.

I To reduce levels of sick leave among officers (one in six assaults leads to a period of sick leave).

I To avoid the negative effect on the organisation that media coverage has when an officer is killed or seriously injured.

I To avoid the adverse effect on the morale of fellow officers.

I Pressure from the rank-and-file officers through the Police Federation.

I Increasing dangers from body fluid infection from high risk groups.

I Empathy for the problems faced by patrol officers.

These changes have been most difficult for chief officers who have striven to change their corporate image from a police **force** to a police **service**. For them, policies of community policing and multi-agency co-operation are not helped by the deployment of officers wearing body armour and carrying batons.

Whatever the reasons for the change, society is witnessing a departure from the non-aggressive police officer personified by Dixon of Dock Green. The image of the police officer today is not one which many actually wanted, rather it has evolved through necessity.

Many observers may see these changes as the end of the 'friendly Bobby'. The danger is that the police become so remote that they cease to appear approachable to the public. However even overtly armed officers at airports find that travellers still speak to them regardless of their body armour and firearms.

The hope is that while the equipment of the British police officer changes, so too will the public's perception and acceptance of the altered image; the ordinary members of the public will still regard themselves and the police as being 'on the same side'.

For although officers may be dressed, equipped and trained differently, the transformation has not been accompanied by any radical change in legislation. Essentially, police officers are still citizens in uniform with limited powers, there are few functions they perform which could not be carried out by the average citizen.

Obviously, the difference is that police officers are the experts and have virtually monopolised the use of legitimate force on the streets. In certain circumstances officers are duty-bound to intervene in hazardous situations where the use of force can be expected.

In such circumstances, the police must be able to ensure their own protection. The public cannot be expected to turn to the police for help if the police cannot even safeguard themselves.

REASONABLE FORCE

Every action police officers take must be 'reasonable' as there is no special protection in law for them using force. Officers must comply with section 3 of the Criminal Law Act 1967:

'A person may use such force as is reasonable in the circumstances in the prevention of crime or in the effecting or assisting in the lawful arrest of offenders or suspected offenders or of persons unlawfully at large.'

There are other provisions which permit officers to use force, such as section 117 of the Police and Criminal Evidence Act 1984 to ensure compliance with the Act, eg, when searching someone. The exercise of force can also be lawful under common law.

Police officers are accountable not only to criminal and civil law, but also to the Police Discipline Code. Any excessive use of force can have far-reaching repercussions for the community. The Rodney King case and the Los Angeles riots that followed, bear testimony to that.

POLICING BY CONSENT

The danger of presenting an all-powerful image to the public is that the police lose the so-called 'British police advantage'. Public sympathy and support have been earned through non-violent and non-confrontational policing methods.

Compliance with police instructions has rarely been achieved by resorting to the use of force. Traditionally compliance has been gained by 'beatcraft': ie, tact, guile and humour. The carrying of equipment such as batons offers greater protection, but poses a serious threat if they are snatched from officers by violent suspects. If officers do not change their beatcraft techniques when dealing with members of the public, especially volatile ones, their personal safety will be put at risk.

A professional approach must be adopted – the price of amateurism could be officers' lives.

PUBLIC SAFETY

The first duty of the police officer is to preserve life. The safety of the public is of prime importance and an historic duty pre-dating Sir Robert Peel's Metropolitan Police Act of 1829. Intelligent use of discretion should be combined with this duty.

In practice, this may mean turning a blind eye to a minor offence on a busy Saturday night in the town centre rather than confronting it head on. While alien to the police sub-culture of action and excitement, the instinct to get involved must be secondary to the issue of public safety. Ill-considered or impulsive action could put officers' safety at risk, and ultimately the safety of the public.

The fatalistic approach taken by some officers – 'Being assaulted occasionally comes with being a police officer' – is unacceptable. In no other occupation (apart from prize fighting) do people accept that being assaulted is inevitable. Some injuries, maybe the majority, are preventable.

Therefore assessing a situation and balancing the dual responsibilities to the public's safety and the officer's safety, is one of the most valuable Street Survival Skills which can be learnt.

STREET SURVIVAL SKILLS

Officer survival falls into three categories:

I Professional Survival.

I Emotional Survival.

I Physical Survival.

If officers are dismissed for committing disciplinary offences, they have not survived **professionally**.

If officers suffer mental breakdowns due to the stress of policework, they have not survived **emotionally**.

This book concentrates on **physical survival**, ie, street survival. Officers can develop their abilities in five areas, called Street Survival Skills.

I ASSESSMENT – Weigh up situations intelligently.

I COMMUNICATION – Communicate effectively.

I SEARCH – Conduct body searches safely.

I ARREST – Carry out arrests safely.

I ESCORT – Transport prisoners safely.

The above list covers the major areas which generate most risks for police officers. By developing skills in each category, officers will be able to reduce the risk of physical injury to themselves.

Obviously, every incident is different, and the above list is not intended to be a programmed response which must be followed slavishly.

Many incidents will begin with an assessment and end with the escort of a suspect from the scene to a police station. Alternatively, an officer may be escorting a detainee from his cell when he suddenly pulls out a knife – a development which may require the officer to assess and communicate.

Essentially, these Street Survival Skills, should be regarded as tools in a mechanic's tool kit. Police officers may not need them all, or in any particular order, but knowing they have them at their disposal should give them greater confidence and ultimately make their job safer.

The distance between police officers and potential assailants differs in the Street Survival Skills. Assessment and communication are non-contact skills whereas search, arrest and escort are skills which require physical contact.

Assessment

Communication

Search

Arrest

Escort

For example, a police officer receives a radio call about an incident several miles away, upon which he or she then starts to make an assessment. At the scene the officer will still be making an assessment as more information is absorbed. Almost certainly the officer will be using communication skills (whilst keeping a safe distance from the individual or individuals concerned). The officer will be in physical contact when he or she searches, arrests and escorts.

Readers may know officers who are already proficient in assessing situations and communicating with volatile personalities to diffuse aggressive behaviour. Readers may also know other officers who are effective at arrest techniques and safe prisoner handling, but seem to jump in with both feet without assessing the situation or trying to communicate properly. Police officers need the full range of Street Survival Skills to do their job effectively and safely.

OVERVIEW

Before the Street Survival Skills are described in detail there are certain basic requirements which readers must be aware of. The concept of survival awareness is necessary to ensure officers act without hesitation in situations of conflict. Tactics like 'contact and cover' may be new to some officers, but are essential when dealing with individuals. The chapter 'Back to basics' covers these issues.

Once the basics have been covered this book concentrates on the five Street Survival Skills, ie, assessment, communication, search, arrest and escort.

The first skill area, assessment, is split into two chapters. The first chapter describes the theory of assessing incidents, the second applies the skill of assessment to some common policing problems which contain a high risk of assaults.

Before the three chapters on the contact skills (search, arrest and escort) are covered there is a need for readers to review the use of force. The 'Use of force' chapter also details the need for officers to be able to explain their reasons for the use of force in writing.

The most serious assaults on police officers are committed with edged weapons and firearms. The 'Weapon threat' chapter provides an overview of the types of firearms officers may encounter; as well as the immediate actions officers should take when dealing with incidents involving weapons.

Following on from the 'Weapon threat' chapter is the 'First aid' chapter which describes the emergency aid for casualties who have sustained wounds. First aid skills are essential to preserve the lives of injured colleagues until professional medical attention is available.

Good physical conditioning is an essential part of officer survival. 'Survival of the fittest' is a chapter concentrating on the benefits of physical fitness for the demanding role of operational police work.

There is a need for readers to have a sound knowledge of the factors involved in assaults on police officers. The 'Dangerous streets' chapter is devoted to an analysis of the circumstances of police assaults.

To many people, officer safety merely equates to assaults on police officers and most of this book is dedicated to those areas where officers can reduce the risk of being assaulted. However, the danger involved in police driving should not be understated. Many more police officers lose their lives in motor vehicle accidents than die due to being assaulted. The 'Police driving' chapter covers those guidelines involved in response and pursuit driving.

SUMMARY

Officer safety is, primarily, an individual responsibility as professional police officers.

To reduce the risks on patrol officers must have:

I *Survival awareness so they can act without hesitation in dangerous situations.*

I *Physical conditioning to perform well in confrontations.*

I *The knowledge of the Street Survival Skills.*

I *An open mind to reflect on their performance and continuously develop.*

Chapter two

BACK TO BASICS

Keypoints

Use this chapter to find out:

I *The three elements of survival.*

I *The fatal errors that place officers at risk of injury.*

I *The states of survival awareness.*

I *The tactical concepts of the reactionary gap, relative positioning, contact and cover, body posture, the 'plus one' rule, and arrest/handcuff then search.*

I *The pre-patrol routine and equipment maintenance regime, including the importance of projecting a professional image.*

Chapter two

Back to Basics

INTRODUCTION

Having basic survival knowledge, as well as appropriate protective equipment and training, are more important than ever in today's policing environment.

The objective of this chapter is to cover basic officer survival concepts, such as contact and cover, which are used when interviewing individuals on the street.

This chapter will also detail routines prior to patrol which will ensure that police officers' protective equipment is fully functional. Going through this routine will reinforce the right mental attitude towards safety on duty.

THE ELEMENTS OF SURVIVAL

There are three elements in surviving an assault:

▌ AWARENESS – Mental preparation including the will to survive.

▌ FITNESS – The physical strength and endurance to win.

▌ DEVELOPMENT – Constantly improving street survival skills.

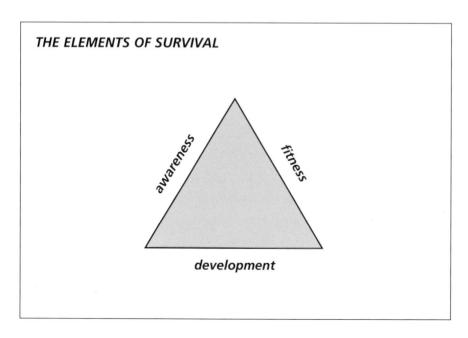

THE ELEMENTS OF SURVIVAL

FATAL ERRORS

Every officer killed on duty may have said to themselves, 'It will never happen to me'. When confronted with a life-threatening situation officers must have the will to win as coming second is coming nowhere. One of the most valuable things police officers can do is to mentally prepare themselves for such an encounter. If assaulted – never give in, even if injured. This survival will is built through **desire**, **belief** and finally **certainty**:

I DESIRE – to live for your own sake and for the people who care about you.

I BELIEF – that you have the skills, equipment and attitude to survive.

I CERTAINTY – that you will survive.

Police officers need to recognise the common pitfalls which have lead to fellow colleagues being killed:

I COMPLACENCY – A complacent attitude can seriously damage police officers' health. Officers may become lulled into such an attitude because patrol work eventually becomes so routine that they miss cues which indicate danger. The police sub-culture can lead officers to become cynical and disillusioned.

I IMPETUOUS HEROISM – Police officers are not indestructible; so why do some rash act in an effort to resolve a dangerous situation quickly? Wait for assistance to arrive instead of acting hastily.

I LACK OF AWARENESS – Look for danger signs (after all police officers are paid to be suspicious) and react. Officers need to pay attention to the hands of people they are interviewing. If officers are going to be attacked it is likely that the assailant will use his or her hands to do it. Stay alert throughout encounters with people – don't switch off.

I NO RESTRAINT – Police officers need to restrain people they search or arrest. When searching keep hold of the person's hands or wrists so that if he moves to attack his intentions will have been signalled to the officer. Handcuff prisoners correctly.

I NO SEARCH – Searches must be systematic and thorough. Officers may feel embarrassed about conducting thorough body searches, but for everyone's safety it must be done properly.

STATES OF SURVIVAL AWARENESS

After a few years of operational policework most situations can become 'routine'. The repetitive nature of the work can lull officers into a dangerous state of complacency.

Most police recruits are 'nice' people. Readers were probably selected because they come from decent backgrounds; they are not prone to sudden outbursts of aggressive behaviour. The police service saw in the readers an aptitude to be calm, rational, professional police officers.

Some people whom the readers have to deal with are fundamentally different. They have found that they are more effective in getting what they want from life by using force rather than reason. They are street wise.

As well as carrying the right equipment and being physically fit, readers need to have mental conditioning to survive. To deal with the street wise they need to raise their state of survival awareness so that they can react without hesitation when faced with a threat.

There are five states of survival awareness:

I WHITE – Officers' minds are in neutral. This is the lowest state of awareness. They are blasé and unaware of their environment.

I YELLOW – Officers have a general concern for their safety. Although they are relaxed they are also alert, keeping an eye out for potential hazards around them.

I ORANGE – Officers have identified a hazard and are assessing the risk it poses to themselves. Their senses are heightened and their minds are evaluating options.

I RED – Action stations! The officers are still thinking rationally as their bodies respond to the threat. They could be using contact techniques to defend themselves and control an adversary.

I BLACK – Lights out! Officers panic and stop functioning.

Police officers must sustain state yellow whilst patrolling. They move up to state orange when assessing and communicating; and go to state red when necessary to survive a physical encounter.

Officers get hurt if they are in state white or black when they encounter a threat. Imagine a couple of officers are on foot patrol at night and call into a petrol station for a cup of tea in the back room. Not an unrealistic scenario. When the officers emerge from the backroom into the shop do they assume that the situation in the shop is going to be the same as when they went into the back? If the officers are in state white they will drift out into the shop oblivious that an armed robbery is happening! If caught like this, in state white, they could go straight to state black, ie, panic and paralysis.

If the officers were in state yellow they would be alert and would re-enter the shop as if entering for the first time. Their senses would be keen and they would be in a good position to move to orange or red.

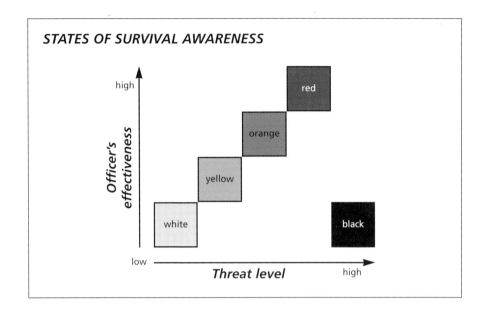

REACTIONARY GAP

To give officers time to react they need a safe distance between themselves and any potential assailant. The circumstances will dictate what is a reasonable distance. Most assaults on police officers are punches, kicks and headbutts. If officers can keep out of the range of potential assailants' fists and feet they can significantly reduce the risk of being assaulted.

Also bear in mind that someone can sprint 20 feet in a little over one second. In normal circumstances two arms' lengths (four to six feet) may be a reasonable distance to maintain.

Police officers can use obstacles, such as a table or fence, to give protection from attack.

Police officers maintain the reactionary gap by instructing the persons they are dealing with to keep back or stand still. It is at the discretion of the police officers to reduce the gap, not the subjects.

When the officers approach people to search or arrest them they lose the protection provided by the reactionary gap so their awareness must increase.

RELATIVE POSITIONING – THE CLOCK SYSTEM

The clock system is used by firearms officers to describe their position in relation to a target. This is the system which will be used in this book to describe various positions around the people officers are interviewing, searching or arresting. The readers need to imagine they are looking down on a person from above then simply superimpose a clock face around them. *'Twelve o'clock'* is directly in front of the person; *'six o'clock'* is directly behind them; *'three o'clock'* is on their right; and, *'nine o'clock'* is on their left.

This system can also be applied to vehicles and buildings.

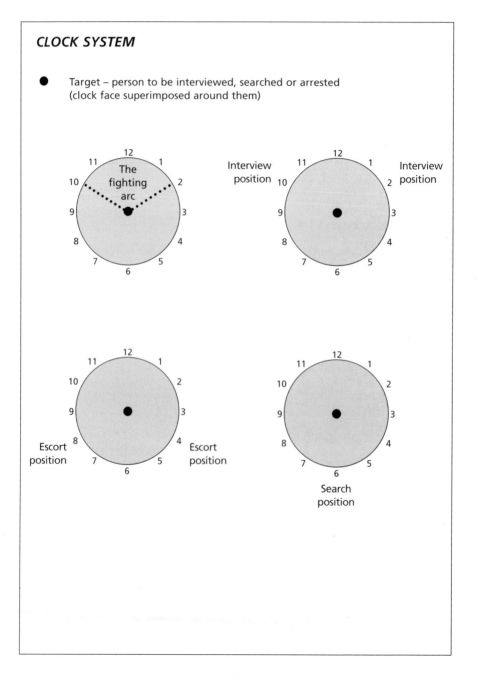

CLOCK SYSTEM

● Target – person to be interviewed, searched or arrested (clock face superimposed around them)

The Fighting Arc

Standing directly in front of another person is the most dangerous position for an officer to stand. Keep out of this fighting arc which extends from *ten o'clock* to *two o'clock*.

The Interview Position

When communicating with an individual keep a reactionary gap and take up the interview position, ie, *ten o'clock* or *two o'clock*. If the person turns to face the officer, verbal commands must be used and the officer needs to keep moving to keep out of the individual's fighting arc.

The Escort Position

When police officers are escorting prisoners – they need to keep behind them at all times. Even if an individual is not under arrest and an officer is walking with him, say to his car, the officer can lightly pat him on the lower back in a friendly manner, this is a positive piece of non-verbal communication; the rear waistband is also a common hiding place for concealed weapons.

The Search Position

To enhance officer safety, conduct body searches from the *six o'clock* position, ie, directly behind the individual.

The fighting arc or 'inside' position.

The interview position.

The escort position.   *The search position.*

Strong Side/Weak Side

A person's strong side is the half of their body with which they would normally launch an attack, this is their dominant side. Nine out of ten people are right-handed – the right is the strong side.

People usually have their wrist watch on their weak side and their trouser belt end points to their weak side. They gesture most often with their strong side hand.

CONTACT AND COVER

The Contact and Cover tactic should be used whenever there are two or more police officers and one or more unsecured individuals. An individual is considered secure when he or she has been handcuffed and searched.

Police officers use contact and cover when they:

▎ Conduct a field interview.

▎ Perform a stop and search.

▎ Make an arrest.

▎ Attend any potentially violent incident.

Whenever the officers' state of awareness is raised due to the behaviour which others adopt they need to employ contact and cover tactics.

Contact and cover.

The principle of this tactic is that one officer adopts the role of *'contact'* and interacts with the individual. The other officer becomes *'cover'* and monitors the scene. Contact and cover enables officers to keep a tactical advantage over any potential assailant.

The contact officer must:

I Ensure his or her own safety.

I Brief the cover officer.

I Conduct the interview and record details.

I Gather intelligence and evidence.

I Handle routine radio messages.

I Perform body or vehicle searches.

I Effect handcuffing and arrest techniques.

The cover officer must:

I Ensure the safety of him/herself and the contact officer.

I Know what the contact officer wants them to do.

I Monitor the environment for hazards.

I Concentrate on the individual(s).

I Discourage fight or flight responses in the individual(s).

I Detect suspicious activity.

I Warn the contact officer of any hostile or suspicious activity seen.

I Not become distracted.

I Be ready to protect him/herself or the contact officer.

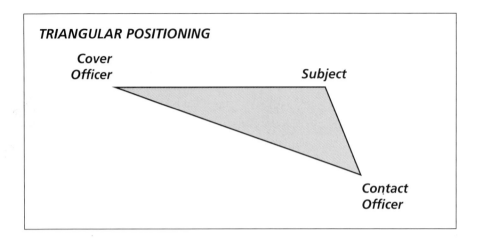

TRIANGULAR POSITIONING

Cover Officer

Subject

Contact Officer

The contact and cover officers should not stand side-by-side. They are safer and more effective if they adopt triangular positioning.

BODY POSTURE

Action is quicker than reaction, so the stance police officers adopt when interviewing people must allow them to:

I Keep their balance.

I Defend themselves immediately with their hands.

I Communicate without appearing aggressive.

The Open Stance

When interviewing:

I Police officers should keep their feet shoulder width apart and point their weak side foot towards the individual.

I They need to keep their weight evenly balanced.

I They should turn their body so their weak side is nearest to the individual. This is a stronger defensive position than facing someone square on. The officer's handcuffs should also be partly concealed from the individual so that they can be drawn covertly.

I The officer's hands should be ready for defensive action. There are several positions available to keep the hands open and above the waist. Officers should adopt a stance which looks and feels natural, but they should not have their hands in their pockets or their arms folded tightly. This only increases the reaction time. If officers can keep their forearms in contact with their baton and handcuffs it will prevent anyone attempting to remove them without the officers' noticing.

The palms open position gives a non-threatening message as the individual can see there is nothing in the officer's hands.

Arms crossed position can appear defensive. The arms are ready for defensive action if they are not folded tightly.

The 'Thinker' position gives an empathetic message as the officer's head is bowed forwards slightly. It also appears as if the officer is listening intently to what the individual is saying.

The prayer or 'Father Murphy' position. The palms are open and facing upwards in a non-threatening manner.

The Defensive Stance

When the reactionary gap is reduced adopt the defensive stance.

Essentially, in the defensive stance, the police officers' hands are raised to shoulder height with their open palms facing towards the individual. By keeping the weak arm fully extended officers can:

▌ Deter a would be attacker from approaching.

▌ Defend themselves by slapping down an attacker's arm.

The raised and open weak hand is a powerful defensive visual sign which is demonstrated in the series of three photographs below and right.

A bystander would probably perceive that the male is the aggressor in this scenario.	*In this photograph the male is still acting aggressively and the officer is using a baton strike. To a bystander this could appear as if both parties were aggressive.*

Remember the importance of the defensive weak hand as demonstrated in the last picture as 'operational policing is a spectator event' (P Boatman).

THE 'PLUS ONE' RULE

When searching, be thorough. The 'plus one' rule is used by determined officers when searching persons, vehicles or buildings. If one object is found suspect the presence of another:

The officer is now using a defensive weak hand gesture. She can still use her baton, but the weak hand gives the appearance of a supplicant gesture as well as the ability to block a punch. A bystander would perceive correctly that the male was the aggressor and the officer was defending herself from attack.

I If a police officer finds one wrap of heroin on an individual he or she keeps searching for another wrap, and so on.

I If one weapon is found in a car, the officer keeps searching for another weapon.

I If one suspect is found in a building, the officer keeps searching for another suspect.

Always assume that there is more to find. It is good practice to always be slightly dissatisfied if nothing is found on a search. It does not mean that evidence is not there, just that it was not found.

When officers conduct searches under section 1 of the Police and Criminal Evidence Act 1984, they need to have formed a 'reasonable suspicion'. This may limit the scope of a search. If reasonable suspicion limits a search to a specific pocket, for example, and the officer found nothing in that pocket he or she would not be justified in continuing the search using the 'plus one' rule.

ARREST/HANDCUFF THEN SEARCH

Some individuals are arrested following a search. Most arrests, however, are not the result of searches as there are already sufficient grounds to arrest. Wherever possible:

I Arrest and handcuff **before** searching (Providing of course that there are grounds to justify handcuffing).

I Do not unhandcuff a prisoner until he or she has been thoroughly searched.

EQUIPMENT FOR PATROL OFFICERS

Before going out on patrol, whether on foot or in a vehicle, it is essential that police officers take the right equipment and that it is fully functional. Confidence can be instilled if this routine is performed prior to patrol. When officers reach for their handcuffs they need to be sure that they are well maintained and will work first time.

Most forces now issue officers with a duty, or utility, belt which is designed to be worn outside the trouser or skirt belt. It may also be attached to a blouson jacket or body armour if this is issued. The duty belt carries most of the protective equipment required on patrol.

The following items are normally carried on the belt:

I Rigid handcuff and holster worn on the strong side (ie on the right for right-handed officers).

I Small torch and pouch.

I Personal medical protection kit in pouch.

I Personal radio and pouch.

I Baton and holder usually worn on the weak side (ie on the left for right handed officers).

I Belt keepers if issued (attached to uniform belt).

I Incapacitant spray and holder (when issued).

Apart from these items officers must have at least one handcuff key and, if issued, wear body armour. Officers should understand the protection level afforded by the body armour. Read and follow the manufacturer's instructions for the care regime for the body armour. The protection afforded by Kevlar is degraded if it is exposed to direct sunlight or soaked. However good the body armour is it will be of no use left hanging in a locker!

Footwear should be lightweight with a good sole which should, ideally, afford protection for the toes and ankles.

If officers are issued with knife resistant gloves they should wear them as much as possible as they will probably not have time to put them on if they are attacked.

When on vehicle patrol officers should have a first aid kit, including a blood spillage pack and a large rechargeable torch in the vehicle. The vehicle should contain sufficient equipment to protect officers at the scene of an accident.

I Do you have signs, cones and lamps? Are they functional?

I Do you have a high visibility jacket?

I Some vehicles carry body armour and riot control helmets. Have you ever tried them on?

PRE-PATROL ROUTINE

Prior to patrol, safety conscious officers ensure that all of their protective equipment is fully functional by adopting a routine.

One such routine is as follows:

I BELT KEEPERS – Unfasten the four belt keepers which are already on the uniform belt (two at the hips and two at the rear) these are needed to secure the duty belt while patrolling and help keep the equipment in place on the belt.

I DUTY BELT – Clip on the duty belt over the uniform belt and ensure that the equipment pouches are on the correct side of the body, such as the rigid handcuff on the strong side and the baton normally on the weak side. The duty belt is then fixed in position outside the uniform belt by fastening the keepers.

I RIGID HANDCUFFS – Check the rigid handcuffs. Draw them from the holster. Push the single bar through the double bar and pull it back to the quick setting (also called the pre-load position). Do the same for both cuffs. Re-holster the handcuffs correctly. It is essential always to carry at least one handcuff key to release the cuff if it is applied too tightly.

I BATON – Ensure the baton is in the correct position and is properly secured in its holster or ring. If the baton is a friction lock type check that it is fully functional by 'racking' it open. Close and holster it.

I TORCH – Ensure that the torch operates correctly. Switch it off and secure it in the pouch.

I PERSONAL MEDICAL PROTECTION POUCH – This should contain a resuscitation aid, surgical gloves, antiseptic wipes and a contaminated waste bag. If any item is missing it should be replaced quickly. A pair of latex gloves costs a few pence and provides an effective barrier between an officer and potential infection.

I PERSONAL RADIO – Check the personal radio for signs of misuse, ie, obvious damage or switches missing. Select a battery and ensure it is fully charged. Assemble the radio and switch on. Check the radio is on the correct channel and do a radio check. Place the radio in the holster and fasten it. If fitted with a handset ensure that the lead will not prevent the drawing of the baton or other equipment. Take care to check the condition of the battery midway through the shift and change it if necessary. If an officer discovers that a radio is unserviceable it must be reported rather than returned to stock. Failure to do so could put a colleague's life at risk!

■ INCAPACITANT SPRAY – Check the unit for signs of damage and secure it in the pouch.

■ BODY ARMOUR – Follow the manufacturer's instructions.

Should any signs of body fluid contamination be found when checking the equipment, eg, blood on the handcuffs, this should be treated immediately. Follow the local force policy on decontamination.

PROJECTING A PROFESSIONAL IMAGE

The image police officers project affects the way other people perceive them; the message officers should be trying to project is that of professionalism. By reviewing their image against the following factors officers should be able to identify any areas for improvement.

■ UNIFORM – A high standard of turnout shows pride in the uniform.

■ HAIR (Males) – What message does a 'skinhead' haircut communicate? The dictionary definition is, 'violent young hooligan'. This is contrary to the professional image officers are trying to project. Police officers with such short hair styles will not intend their appearance to be 'thuggish', but it may well be perceived as such by others.

■ HAIR (Females) – Loose hair can obscure vision and pony tails can be a disadvantage if attacked.

■ JEWELLERY – Large rings, bracelets, necklaces or earrings can cause injury. Unofficial tie pins with cartoon animals or bearing slogans, eg, 'Make my day asshole!' are totally inappropriate.

■ PERFUME – As figures of authority the over-use of perfume, cologne or aftershave can send out confusing messages to the public. Over-use of scent will also hinder the investigation of crime, eg, officers may not detect the aroma of certain drugs.

■ HYGIENE – Body odour or bad breath due to a lack of personal hygiene also detracts from an officer's professional image.

■ POSTURE – Whatever your height – walk tall. Stand up straight and do not slouch. Officers can project a confident presence by their bearing.

Readers should take a minute or so to consider how they match up to the above criteria. Readers can sound out someone whose opinion they trust if they have concerns about the image they project.

First impressions count and a police officer's appearance should be that of a serious professional. If officers project an air of confidence others will assume they have the capability to deal with their problems.

PERIODIC EQUIPMENT MAINTENANCE

To ensure that the equipment is fully functional carry out the following routines on a periodic basis, eg, on the first early or morning shift of the month.

Torch

The torch should contain a spare bulb in the base cap. Once a month remove and inspect the batteries, replace them when they are weak or showing signs of deterioration (moisture or leakage).

Baton

FRICTION LOCK BATONS – once a month **lightly** lubricate the barrels of the baton and dry off any excess oil. Chromed barrels should not require lubrication. Make sure no oil gets onto the handle.

POLYCARBONATE BATONS – with regular handling the polycarbonate baton develops a film of grease which should be removed by cleaning the baton in soapy water and rinsing it thoroughly.

Rigid handcuffs

Once a month inspect and carry out the following checks.

1 Visually check the handcuff for any signs of body fluid contamination. If contamination is found treat in an approved manner.

2 Push the single bar through the double bar, then pull it back to the preload or quick setting.

3 Check that the single bar is in line with the cheek plates either side of the ratchet, ie, the single bar has not become twisted.

4 Push in the double locking pin and check that the single bar is locked. You can use the tip of a ball-point pen to push the double locking pin in rather than rummage for a handcuff key, **but remember always to carry at least one handcuff key**.

5 Turn the key AWAY from the double bar and check that the double locking pin returns to the off position.

6 Turn the key TOWARDS the double bar and check that the single bar moves freely.

7 Repeat this process with the other cuff.

8 Lightly oil the moving parts (ie, the boss and the ratchet bar area) of the handcuffs with a moisture displacing lubricant, WD40 or AC90 are recommended.

9 Check the cuffs for ease of operation and wipe any excess oil from the metallic parts. Ensure that the rigid handcuff grip is completely dry.

10 Reset the handcuffs to the preload setting.

11 Re-holster the handcuffs correctly.

TRAINING

Manufacturers of protective equipment have approved training pro-grammes associated with their equipment. The successful completion of an approved training course is signified by a certificate. The training course will be founded on medical, legal and practical research. This training needs to be periodically updated. Whilst using a piece of equipment with the correct training and using an approved technique officers will be supported by the manufacturer should a relevant issue arise in court. If police officers let their training lapse, use an incorrect technique, or modify the equipment they will probably be on their own in any court proceedings.

It is only with regular practice that police officers can hope to master the techniques used in self-defence and other equipment, such as baton and handcuffs.

The message is quite clear. Police officers must ensure that their author-ity to use equipment remains up to date. As they approach the end of their authorised period officers should make sure that they receive refresher training. Only approved techniques should be used and the equipment should not be modified in any way as this may invalidate the manufacturer's obligations.

SUMMARY

▮ Beware of the fatal errors which can lead to officers being injured. The worst error is complacency.

▮ Constantly practice maintaining an appropriate state of awareness.

▮ Keep a safe reactionary gap from individuals.

▮ Adopt the safest position relative to an individual, remembering to keep out of the fighting arc.

▮ Use contact and cover tactics.

▮ Project a professional image.

▮ Arrest and handcuff before searching.

▮ Search thoroughly using the 'plus one' rule.

▮ Adopt a pre-patrol routine by checking each piece of equipment thoroughly.

▮ Regularly maintain equipment to ensure serviceability.

Chapter three

ASSESSMENT SKILLS – THEORY

Keypoints

Use this chapter to find out:

▮ *What factors are considered when assessing situations.*

▮ *The relevance of a sound assessment when deciding on the best course of action.*

Chapter three

Assessment Skills – Theory

THE NEED FOR ASSESSMENT SKILLS

There appears to be a scarcity of information on assessing common operational policing situations. In certain specialised operations, such as firearms incidents, officers use decision-making processes similar to military 'combat appreciations'. These assess the factors involved in a given incident, create options and decide on the best option. Past experience helps police officers approach incidents intelligently. Sometimes though officers can still get drawn into a 'bad' situation even after years of experience.

Have you ever ended up in an incident where you wish you could have turned the clock back a few minutes and have said to yourself, 'Why have I got involved in this?' Even after years of trying to approach problems shrewdly, police officers can still end up in messy situations where the only options are bad ones.

Imagine a team of officers on van patrol in the town centre at night when a group of a dozen or so boisterous men pass by on their way home. When the group are almost out of earshot one shouts something abusive towards the van. Unable to identify which man shouted at the van the officers, nevertheless, intercept the group who are now on waste ground some distance from the town centre. A stand off occurs. Some of the men are ready to 'square up' to the police while others are trying to calm things down.

The police officers have almost engineered this problem. By pursuing the men, who are on their way home anyway, the officers have ended up with a confrontation. To withdraw would be to lose face, but to engage the group would lead to injuries to both sides.

There are no good options and, it could be argued, that from the start reinforcements should have been brought in to deal with the group. Alternatively, the officers could have ignored the original abusive remark. Some assessment at the beginning of the incident might have avoided a stand off.

The decision as to whether officers deal with some incidents depends upon the seriousness of any offences which may have been committed. The writer firmly believes that assessing operational police incidents is crucial to officer safety. This chapter is devoted to an understanding of the theory of the assessment skill. As this book is designed for operational officers the next chapter puts the skill of assessment into practical policing situations. The knowledge readers gain from this chapter will be put to use in the next chapter.

Health and safety training gives a valuable insight into assessing risk. In operational policing terms there can only be two classifications of risk, 'high risk' and 'unknown risk'. Someone threatening an officer with a weapon would be an obvious example of a '**high risk**'. Anyone who appears passive and unarmed can only be an '**unknown risk**'. Any other system of classifying risk can lead to complacency and officers being injured.

If a logical mental framework is applied to policing problems, danger can be minimised. Quite simply the assessment answers the following questions:

I OBJECTIVE – 'What am I trying to achieve here?'

I SUBJECT(S) – 'What danger do the people involved pose to me?'

I ENVIRONMENT – 'What hazards are there nearby?'

I AVAILABLE RESOURCES – 'What can I do about it on my own or with backup?'

Objective　　　　　　　　　　　　*Subject(s)*

'What am I trying to achieve here?'　　　*'What danger do the people involved pose to me?'*

33

Environment   **Available Resources**

'What hazards are there nearby?'   'What can I do about it on my
                                         own or with backup?'

Every assessment considers the **objective**, the **subject(s)**, the
environment, and the **resources**. Readers will already mentally 'weigh up'
a policing problem before they deal with it. This chapter details a mental
approach with which to structure the assessment skill.

Examine each of these components in detail and apply them to the
reality of operational policing situations. Assessing situations should not
be thought of solely as the work of those with the luxury of time to plan
operations.

Assessments can be done, and usually will be done, on the spot when
attending an incident. Ideally an assessment is best made before the police
officers are so close as to be committed to the incident. Assessments are
often made on the approach to the incident. Once embroiled in the
situation the officers' options may have been reduced as they have
committed themselves to a course of action. Assessments may have to be
done rapidly as officers rarely enjoy unlimited preparation time. Incidents
are dynamic and when the factors involved change the situation will need
to be re-assessed quickly.

Assessment is a real life-saving skill as important as any self-defence technique to be learnt and practised continuously. A good assessment may well save officers from serious injury.

THE OBJECTIVE

When assessing operational incidents police officers must base their thinking on their objective. This may all sound like common sense, but how often have officers committed themselves to some trivial incident which has got out of hand and lost sight of the objective they intended to achieve?

There are few professions where an individual's life is at risk in the course of their work – police work is one such profession. There is no merit in risking your life unnecessarily.

When police officers are called upon to justify their actions they should be able to base them on the objective they were setting out to achieve. If officers are clear about their objectives they can communicate them to the people involved in the incident to assist in resolving the situation peacefully.

The overall mission of policing is **public safety**. Whether this is attending a domestic dispute or supervising a football match the safety of the public must be the primary consideration.

There is hardly any activity in society where the police may not have a legitimate interest from a sporting event ranging to computer fraud. Policing objectives are defined to focus policing activities on those areas which are of most concern to the community.

The ACPO Strategic Document has actually spelt out the common purpose of the police service:

'The purpose of the Police Service is to uphold the law fairly and firmly; to prevent crime; to pursue and bring to justice those who break the law; to keep the Queen's Peace; to protect, help and reassure the community; and to be seen to do all this with integrity, common sense and sound judgement.

We must be compassionate, courteous and patient, acting without fear or favour or prejudice to the rights of others. We need to be professional, calm and restrained in the face of violence and apply only such force which is necessary to accomplish our lawful duty...'.

On an operational policing level on what do officers base their activities? In the real world police officers reduce their objectives to a mental set of priorities on which they base their day to day work.

A police officer's personal 'top five' priorities may look something like this:

▮ Survive unharmed.

▮ Prevent harm to others.

▮ Attend emergencies promptly.

▮ Intervene in disorders to restore order.

▮ Detect crime and arrest offenders.

There are of course other factors, the most important being discretion. Whether or not police officers intervene in an incident and to what extent they intervene will be based on the discretion they use. The objective for a particular incident will be dependent upon what the officers want to achieve.

'What is it that I want to achieve in this incident?' If officers attend an address to execute a 'fail to appear' court warrant the objective will be the arrest of the subject.

'What will a successful outcome look like?' A successful outcome of executing an arrest warrant will be that none of the police officers involved are injured and the subject is arrested.

Can you apply this to a police pursuit as easily?

Police officers need to have a clear picture in their minds of what the objective is in intervening in a situation. Now assess the factors posed by, the subject(s); the environment; and, the available resources. Once this is accomplished look at what options are open before deciding on the best course of action.

THE SUBJECT(S)

An individual with the motivation, opportunity and capability to cause harm.

Assess the subject for Motivation, Opportunity and Capability to cause harm. Consider:

I MOTIVATION – 'Does this person **want** to harm me?'

I OPPORTUNITY – 'Has this person a **chance** of harming me?'

I CAPABILITY – 'Does this person possess the **ability** to harm me?'

If the answer to one or more of these questions is, 'Yes' or 'Not known' then police officers should consider treating the subject as **high risk**.

Motivation

People are motivated to assault police officers by one or more of the four Ds:

I DRUNK – The influence of excessive alcohol consumption.

I DRUGGED – Substance misuse, either controlled drugs or solvents.

I DESPERATE – To avoid arrest at all costs due to the seriousness of the offence or the effect an arrest would have on their lives.

I DISTURBED – Either mentally disordered or emotionally angry.

Opportunity

The opportunity to assault officers presents itself in the following ways:

I **Proximity** of the potential assailant to the officer.

I Any **weapons** to which the person has access.

I The **number** of people present.

I Where the other person has the advantage of **surprise**.

Capability

The potential for another person to assault officers will also depend upon their capability:

I **Age**.

I **Gender**.

I **Build** (height and weight) relative to the officer.

I **Ability**, or apparent ability, in combative skills, such as boxing or martial arts.

I **Warning signals** if known (from PNC).

- **Antecedents** (criminal history).
- **Ailments**, particularly contagious diseases, eg hepatitis.

Officers will form their initial assessment of the subject on the following:

- The subjects' behaviour (abusive, aggressive, drunk, drugged, deranged).
- Their previous dealings with him or her (if any).
- Information from databases, such as PNC.
- Third party information. The control room operator may tell officers the source of the information, eg, other police officers, neighbours, etc.
- The police officer's own observations. The officer may see a weapon being carried by the subject or the subject may look nervous and reach into a pocket on seeing the officer possibly indicating that he or she has a concealed weapon.
- The officer's professional knowledge of the risks inherent in certain operational incidents (see the next chapter).

Remember to re-assess the incident if any of the factors change.

THE ENVIRONMENT

Objectively assess the environment.

- Firstly, as the primary duty of the police is public safety, ask yourself, 'Are there any innocents or potential victims nearby?'
- Secondly, 'What are the risks posed by the hazards in the vicinity?'

A 'hazard' is a potential danger to your safety or the safety of others. A 'risk' is the possibility of that hazard actually causing harm.

A large ferocious dog locked in a car would be a 'hazard'. The 'risk' is the chance that someone might let it out of the car.

Other hazards in the environment might include:

- The presence of **associates** of the subject.
- **Bystanders** becoming involved in the situation.
- Any kind of **weapon**, such as beer glasses.
- Anything which could be used to cause injury, examples of these could be vehicles or dogs.
- Any other physical **hazard**, passing traffic, shop windows, etc.

TACTICAL THINKING

When assessing a policing problem think tactically. Sort out the factors into:

I Problem areas.

I Areas of responsibility.

I Focus point.

TACTICAL THINKING

> **Problem areas**

> **Areas of responsibility**

> **Focus point**

Problem Area

A problem area is anything which contains a risk of being a hazard. It could be:

I A **person**.

I An **object**.

I A **location**.

An incident with a drunken man holding a broken beer bottle outside a pub presents three obvious problem areas; drunken man (person), broken beer bottle (object), and pub (location).

Areas of Responsibility

Anywhere an attack may come from is an area of responsibility. The drunken man's hands, feet, head and the broken bottle are areas of responsibility, so is the door from the pub from which other people may appear.

Police officers need to identify and control the areas of responsibility in any incident.

Focus Point

The primary threat to an officer should become the focus point. The drunken man's broken beer bottle may be the point an officer needs to focus on immediately in this scenario.

Officers should ask themselves:

❗ Where are the problem areas?

❗ What are the areas of responsibility here?

❗ How can I control the areas of responsibility?

❗ What is my focus point?

Assess the environment in a logical order. Take a room for example.

A room with three areas of responsibility.

There are three areas of responsibility; the subject in the room, an open door, and a closed door. It is obvious that an officer's safety may be at risk from the person in the room; the officer will have already assessed the 'subject' by this stage. The next area of responsibility is the potential of a hazard emerging from another room, for example another person who is yet to enter the room. The officer's second priority is therefore to cover any open door through which a potential assailant may rush into the room. The third area of responsibility is the closed door, the officer will need to take precautions to ensure that it can be covered in case it is opened and someone else enters the room.

Is the environment one which can be contained until the arrival of rein- forcements? An example of this could be a room with only one exit.

AVAILABLE RESOURCES

The last part of the assessment is the resources available to the police officer, such as:

I The **number of police officers** or others to assist.

I Any **specialist officers** available, eg dog handlers, PSU, ARV, etc.

I The police officer's own **age, weight, build and gender** relative to the person(s) he or she is encountering.

I The **officer's relative fitness, skill and level of fatigue** compared to that of the subject. Including any disability the officer may be suffering from.

I **Protective equipment** available.

I The **time available** to deal with the incident.

I Whether or not the officer has the element of **surprise**.

OPTIONS

Police officers' options will be influenced by their own objectives, the subject, the environment, and their resources. Whether or not they can use discretion on intervening depends largely upon the seriousness of the incident.

The following courses of action may be considered:

I Do nothing at the time (use discretion if appropriate in the circumstances) –
'Is it essential that the person is arrested at this time?'
'Can he or she be easily found at a later date?'
'Is evidence likely to be lost by delaying action?'

OR

I Act immediately (maintain surprise and move in to engage the subject). Action is quicker than reaction, so if police officers take the initiative and surprise the individuals by handcuffing them without warning they may well succeed.

OR

I Begin communication keeping a safe reactionary gap.

OR

I Await support (reinforcements and/or supervision).

Select the best course and act upon it. If there are other officers involved they will have to communicate with each other so they know the plan of action.

It is often a good idea for officers to let their colleagues know that they intend to act, eg, by arresting the subject, without tipping the individual off until the arrest is made. This can be done with a codeword between officers or some non-verbal action like covertly unclipping the handcuff holster strap.

One successful tip is for one officer to deliberately call his or her colleague using an incorrect first name. This will alert the colleague and raise their state of survival awareness without giving warning to anyone else. The first thing the subject should know is that an officer is snapping handcuffs on him and informing him that he is under arrest. The fellow officer will have known that some action was imminent and will have been prepared for any reaction. The point of arrest is often a 'flashpoint' for assaulting police officers; once an officer has laid hands on the arrested person he is faced with a dilemma for which there are three options:

I FIGHT – Assault the officer.

I FLIGHT – Try to escape.

I FOLLOW – Comply with the officer's instructions.

SUMMARY

To summarise:

I Assessment is a street survival skill every bit as important as the contact techniques of search, arrest and escort.

I Assessments should be done before an officer gets involved in the incident.

I When factors change, re-assess the incident.

I Consider the objective.

I Observe the subject.

I Observe the environment

I Take stock of available resources.

I Finally, consider which options are open and decide on the best one.

Chapter four

ASSESSMENT SKILLS – PRACTICE

Keypoints

Use this chapter to find out:

I *How assessment skills apply to foot stops, traffic stops, disputes and crimes in progress.*

I *How to prepare for being attacked unexpectedly.*

I *How to recognise the risks involved in these policing activities.*

Chapter four

Assessment Skills – Practice

RESEARCH

The Home Office studied over two hundred incidents in which officers were assaulted (Brown, 1994). These assault situations were categorised, eg, foot stops, traffic stops, etc. These categories are analysed in this chapter using the assessment framework from the last chapter, namely objective, subject, environment and resources. Instead of options, tactical advice is offered.

There are few faultless solutions in hazardous situations. When stopping cars, for example, some officers advise pulling up close behind the other vehicle to minimise the impact in case it rams their vehicle. Others stop two car lengths behind to give themselves time to react. Readers must decide on their best option bearing in mind all the factors involved.

It is important never to treat any situation as 'routine', so always be alert for signs of danger.

There have been incidents where officers have approached cars along the nearside rather than the offside, only to spot the driver holding a gun, waiting for the officer to approach along the predictable offside. Be creative and do the unexpected.

It must be stressed that the incidents described in this chapter are the ones which commonly result in assaults on police. It will be each officer's decision as to which option to take. Tactical advice has been included which may guide readers in the way they deal with these incidents.

FOOT STOPS

Foot stops occur when officers on foot patrol conduct stop checks of people or vehicles.

Objective

I Survive.

I Intercept criminals.

I Gather intelligence.

Subject

Consider what evidence there is to suspect the person of an offence, if any. How serious is the offence? Observe carefully the subject(s) and consider the possible threat they pose. Do they have the motivation, opportunity or capability to cause harm? Some people are motivated to escape arrest, possibly due to incriminating evidence which they are carrying. The person may well attack an officer as soon as the officer begins talking to him or her. Assaults can also often take place as the arrest is made.

Subject on Foot

Assessing a suspect on foot.

Environment

As foot stops are conducted in public places there are risks that others may get involved. In a town centre street the person stopped may be aided by other people. In a residential street, neighbours may assist the subject, especially if the area is 'hard to police'. Once police officers have selected the person they want to stop they should then decide on their approach and the best location for the stop check. Choose the location for

Conducting a stop in a controlled environment.

the stop with care. Ideally the location should close down options for the other person, for example a shop doorway in a street. It should also be chosen to reduce the possibility of other people becoming involved. For example it would be unwise to perform the stop check next to a busy pub, night-club or chip shop, unless necessary.

Tactical Advice – Person on Foot

In cases where the person is suspected of being responsible for a violent crime or possibly armed with an offensive weapon obtain assistance. If the person is on foot it may be best for officers to keep him or her under discreet observation until in a good position for the stop to be carried out.

Shrewd officers close to a safe reactionary gap before announcing to the individual their intention to stop him.

Always be ready for a snap assessment, for example where police officers encounter a likely subject by chance coming around a corner and have to 'think on their feet'.

Readers may have drawn the following conclusions as to the best practice when making a 'foot stop':

I If on solo patrol contact the control room and inform them of the **location**.

I If support is needed ask for **backup**. One officer and one subject are not good odds.

I If possible maintain the **initiative** and wait for the subject to walk away from an obvious hazard, eg, a rowdy pub.

I Direct the subject into a **controlled area**, eg, a recessed doorway.

I **Anticipate** that the subject may attack in an effort to escape arrest.

Only move into close quarters to conduct a search if the subject complies with verbal commands and, ideally, a colleague is in support.

Stopping a Vehicle whilst on Foot Patrol

Stopping vehicles whilst on foot patrol is fraught with danger. Seriously consider, 'Why am I trying to stop this vehicle?' Officers will try to stop vehicles driven by drivers with impaired ability or reckless car thieves. The location for the stop should be chosen with care. At least have a solid refuge near the kerb, such as a mature tree or other solid piece of street furniture, to take cover behind if the driver fails to stop. Ideally the site should allow the driver of the vehicle to see the officer in plenty of time. The free flow of traffic should not be obstructed by the stopped vehicle. Between dusk and dawn wear a fluorescent and reflective jacket, carry a torch and be illuminated by street lighting. The main danger initially is

Stopping a vehicle whilst on foot patrol can be hazardous.

from the ton or so of metal the subject is driving. Officers have been killed when they have had their arm trapped and the vehicle has driven off. The message is clear:

Don't put any part of your body inside a vehicle if there is a risk the vehicle might move.

If it appears that the vehicle is not going to stop – **let it go**.

Own Resources

Research shows that quite often police officers are on their own when conducting a foot stop check.

Tactical Advice

I Consider seriously the risks of trying to stop a vehicle whilst on foot patrol, especially at night.

I Chose the location carefully when planning to stop a vehicle while on foot patrol.

I Consider cover, visibility and lighting.

I If a vehicle is not going to stop – get out of the way.

I Do not become trapped in the vehicle.

TRAFFIC STOPS

Traffic stops are where police officers driving patrol cars stop subjects who are driving or on foot.

Objective

I Survive.

I Public safety – enforcement of traffic laws.

I Interception of criminals.

I Gathering criminal intelligence.

Subject

The Home Office study indicates that drivers who assault police officers are likely to be drunk or desperate to escape. This is more likely the closer they are to their home. They could resort to using weapons, either an article from the vehicle or the vehicle itself. Several officers have been killed by drivers either running them down or dragging them along.

The passengers in a vehicle are more likely to attack officers than the driver. Drivers have legal responsibilities when taking their vehicle on the road, their passengers are less likely to be inhibited by legal niceties. Whilst engaged in interviewing the driver, officers should ask themselves, 'What are the passengers doing?'

If the occupants of the vehicle are drunk their attack could well be persistent. That is, they will assault officers **before**, **during** and **after** their arrest.

Environment

The environmental hazards may be aggravated if the vehicle is stopped where bystanders are likely to intervene. Passing traffic is also hazardous especially if an impaired driver approaches the scene.

Own Resources

Police officers who work as part of a double crewed vehicle should make the best use of their resources by having standard procedures worked out for stopping vehicles.

Tactical Advice

I Consider the location of the stop; away from sources of assistance for the subject (pubs and the subject's home); and on a safe stretch of road.

I If the occupants of the vehicle outnumber the police officers, inform the control room of the location.

I Position the vehicle in the safest manner. Using lights to warn other road users. Try and park the police vehicle closer to the centre of the road to create a safety lane along the offside of the subject's vehicle.

Stopping a vehicle from the rear.

I Leave the headlights on at night whilst the police vehicle passenger (observer) gets out quickly, before the driver or occupants of the other vehicle get out in order to maintain the initiative.

I At night wear a high visibility jacket.

I The observer should approach the subject vehicle carefully and request the driver to switch off the engine. Consider asking the driver to remove the ignition keys and either place them on the dashboard or hand them over.

I The police driver then approaches the rear of the subject's vehicle and will act as the observer's 'cover'. Keeping at the rear of the subject's vehicle allows observation of the occupants of the vehicle and keeps the occupants from knowing exactly where the cover officer is.

I The driver of the subject vehicle is requested by the observer to get out of the vehicle and is interviewed on the nearside pavement.

I The officer explains why he or she stopped the vehicle and the reasons why requests are made, such as the removal of the ignition keys.

I If the vehicle is to be searched it would be safer for all the occupants to stand, or ideally sit down, on the nearside pavement covered by one officer whilst the other conducts a search of the vehicle.

I Officers need to exercise caution in case a subject drives the vehicle at them, either forwards or in reverse trapping the officers against the police vehicle behind. Never cling on to a moving vehicle!

Stopping a Person on Foot

I Either stop along the person's direction of travel giving sufficient time to get safely out of the police vehicle and approach the subject on foot or stop behind the person and approach him from the rear.

▌ Never try to conduct a stop check whilst seated in a vehicle. Police officers are at a disadvantage and provide easy targets for would-be attackers.

Consider stopping well in front of the subject.

Use the vehicle as an obstacle to give protection from the subject.

Avoid getting in between combative individuals.

DISPUTES

Researchers have found that intervening in arguments between individuals is dangerous, especially if the participants are frustrated, aggressive and/or drunk.

Objective

I Survive.

I Public safety must be a primary consideration.

I Restore order.

Subjects

Personal disputes which are fuelled by alcohol lead to aggression often directed at police officers. The people involved are not likely to be acting rationally.

The flashpoints for assaults on police officers in disputes are usually when the officers are refused entry to the premises or when one of the parties is arrested.

Be aware that the headbutt is a common means of delivering an assault in this situation due to the confined space. It is common for other people to join in as 'rescuers'. If two people are fighting when the police arrive they are likely to assault the officers for intervening in their argument. Remember that disputes occur anywhere, not solely in buildings.

Environment

In domestic disputes those involved have an advantage in that they know the location of articles which can be used as weapons.

Where disputes occur in licensed premises the presence of plentiful supplies of glass hazards (beer glasses and bottles) should be considered.

Own Resources

If police officers are not double-crewed when attending a violent dispute extreme caution should be exercised. Wait for backup whenever possible.

Tactical Advice

If there is a fight actually taking place, keep a reactionary gap and use verbal commands to break up the protagonists. It is important for officers to announce clearly, they are the police so that individuals in the dispute cannot later claim that they did not know who they were dealing with.

If one of the subjects is receiving a beating, use verbal commands and consider going into close quarters to deliver a baton strike on the aggressor if this is justified in the circumstances (see Use of Force Chapter). These strikes should be carried out swiftly, moving back each time to re-assess the situation once a reactionary gap has been regained.

Do not try to jump straight into the middle of a fight hoping that the uniform will afford protection from an attack. The reactionary gap is lost when officers move into the middle of a melee and they would be unable to use their batons effectively; they also risk their batons being taken from them with dire consequences!

Ideally all the subjects involved in the dispute should be separated and 'covered' by other officers before moving in to arrest any of them. Develop arrest techniques which enhance officer safety (see Arrest Techniques Chapter).

For potentially violent subjects consider the 'touch'n'cuff' method of arrest. This involves speedy application of a cuff the instant police officers touch the person they are arresting using an approved Quik-Kuf technique. If the person becomes violent at least officers have a control method already applied, ie, a rigid handcuff on one wrist. The subject can then be restrained by applying a control technique to ensure compliance, such as a takedown to prone.

Do not relax once after the arrest has been made.

If there are two subjects who are potentially violent, eg, two partners in a domestic dispute, it is standard practice to separate them. Be careful in these situations as this practice divides police resources.

Always know where the exit is and, wherever possible, never let anyone block the exit route.

Be prepared for a sudden change in behaviour by one person when their partner is arrested. Police officers may be attacked by the 'victim' in the dispute who has experienced a sudden change of heart upon seeing a loved one being arrested.

Handcuffing an apparently placid person in front of a drunken crowd could be seen as a provocative act. People in the crowd may take on the role of 'rescuer' by assaulting the 'persecutor' (the officer) to assist the 'victim' (the arrested person).

If escorting an arrested person out of a building the most dangerous moment occurs when the exit is reached. If the subject is going to make a bid to escape this is his best chance, especially if he has not been handcuffed. It may have been decided not to handcuff the individual in front of other people to prevent an escalation of the situation, eg, in a busy night-club. Anticipate the individual's actions and pre-empt them.

Take the initiative, do not wait for the subject to make their move. Move him into a controlled area like a corner in order to handcuff him before reaching the exit.

INTERRUPTING A CRIME IN PROGRESS

When catching a criminal 'red-handed', expect to be faced with extreme violence. The surprise element gives the police officer little or no time to prepare for the encounter.

Anticipate being faced by resistance when interrupting a crime.

Objective

I Survive.

I Arrest the offender.

Subject

The criminals are likely to be armed with articles which could be used as offensive weapons, especially in burglaries, eg, a screwdriver. They are also likely to take possession of anything at the scene. Offenders are likely to assault police officers the instant they encounter them.

Environment

Crimes in progress could occur literally anywhere from a telephone kiosk to Buckingham Palace. Building searches are especially dangerous. Avoid approaching a building from the obvious route. Always have sufficient officers to search a building safely. Make use of torches and dog handlers if available.

Own Resources

According to the research conducted by the Home Office, police officers could well be alone when encountering these incidents. Due to their spontaneous nature there will be no time to prepare.

Tactical Advice

The worst case scenario would be encountering a team of criminals committing an offence whilst patrolling alone. It may be safer to take up a covert observation point and contact the control room rather than tackle the group immediately. Assume the criminals have radio scanners and will be intercepting police radio messages. Choose a safe location which cannot be easily identified by the radio messages transmitted.

Expect to be met with desperate subjects determined to escape. Be ready to use defensive baton techniques as the criminals will show no inhibitions in assaulting anyone who gets in their way. Criminals' behaviour is not governed by any rule book.

When interrupting sexual offences, such as gross indecency between males, expect violence in the offenders' attempts to escape arrest. The stigma of being arrested for such an offence and the adverse consequences for their job and family may well cause an 'ordinary' man to resort to desperate measures to escape.

THE UNEXPECTED ATTACK

By its very nature police officers cannot assess an unexpected attack; they can, however, have a plan ready. Occasionally officers are assaulted completely out of the blue. **These assaults often result in serious injury!**

Objective

I Preserve life.

I Police officers are no use to the public, their families or their colleagues if injured.

I Arrest offenders if practical.

Subjects

The research shows these to be predominantly male groups motivated to attack officers because of hatred of the police or some 'wrong' the police may have done to them in the past. **Expect the offenders to use weapons**.

Environment

Although these attacks could occur anywhere they are more likely in the 'hard to police' areas where tensions exist between the police and the community.

Own Resources

Police officers will probably be targeted when they are most vulnerable, either on their own or off duty.

Tactical Advice

Officers need to create distance, get an obstacle between themselves and the attacker(s), call for backup and defend themselves tenaciously.

Use force under section 3 of the Criminal Law Act 1967. Bear in mind that these subjects are probably intent on causing serious injury.

When confronted by two or more attackers the best option might be to get into a relative safe area, this could be a doorway or a stairway. If an officer controls a doorway only one person at a time will be able to attack.

Police officers may need to break through the attackers to reach safety. There are no prizes for coming out second best, so officers must have the will to win. When the attackers are about a car length away (15 feet) make eye contact with an attacker on one side of the group, say the right-hand side, then dash towards the opposite side, the left-hand side, to break out.

Break out around the side of the attackers, not through the middle.

Try and bypass the group of attackers by going around the outside of one of them. This will mean that only one potential assailant will be able to attack.

Avoid getting between two attackers to prevent being assaulted from two directions at once. Do not try and kick a way through a group of attackers; it is faster to use empty hand techniques or baton blocks, chops and jabs. Strike the nearest individual's shoulder to knock him or her off balance and towards another attacker.

Once safety has been reached survive until help arrives. Use defensive tactics and baton techniques to keep the attackers away.

Fend off attackers until assistance arrives.

SUMMARY

I Develop skills in assessing these potentially dangerous situations.

I Where certain additional factors exist, such as drunkenness, officers need to increase their level of awareness.

I Police officers should be ready to react immediately to protect themselves, by any reasonable means, when attacked or if interrupting a crime in progress.

Chapter five

COMMUNICATION SKILLS

KEYPOINTS

Use this chapter to find out:

I *The difference between emotional and social aggression.*

I *How to manage anger.*

I *How to use assertive techniques and give verbal commands.*

I *How to use empathy.*

I *How to communicate with the 'awkward customer'.*

Chapter five

Communication Skills

There are times when police officers have no opportunity to communicate with potential assailants before they are committed to engaging them with a self-defence to arrest technique, for example when attacked unexpectedly. However, in most incidents leading to an assault, there is likely to be an opportunity to communicate first.

Research into police assaults (Phillips & Cochrane, 1991) has recommended that officers should possess a variety of skills to deal with high risk incidents. Furthermore they should be trained to resolve conflict in a non-confrontational manner.

Another study (Wilson, 1993) concluded that officers who preferred a 'confrontational approach' met more resistance from individuals than those who adopted a problem solving method. A later study by the same researcher (Wilson, 1994) found that the angrier the officers were the more resistance they met. Interestingly, officers who acted assertively met less resistance.

There is no one ingredient for effective communication. Officers must possess a range of communication strategies and have the flexibility to employ the most appropriate one in the circumstances. The ability to manage anger, act assertively, and employ an empathetic approach which will enable officers to view the situation from the subject's perspective are essential. Some situations will require more than one of these skills.

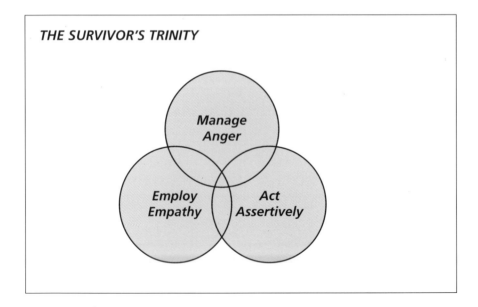

THE SURVIVOR'S TRINITY

Manage Anger

Employ Empathy

Act Assertively

Faced with a group of rowdy football supporters police officers may need both to manage their own anger and to act assertively. In the case of a man who has become enraged in the context of a domestic dispute, officers will need to manage his anger and employ an empathetic approach. The survivor's trinity is a model which can help visualise the three skills involved in communicating effectively at an operational level.

Improving communication skills in these three areas will be a continuous process. When communicating always be aware of personal safety and maintain a safe distance from the subject or have an obstacle in between, say a cell door. Always try to ensure an unobstructed access to an exit and always face the individual.

There are aspects of cross-cultural communication which officers should be aware of. The example usually given is a difference in eye-contact between individuals of different ethnic groups.

Professional officers should increase their knowledge of cross-cultural communication issues with ethnic minority groups in their area.

EMOTIONAL VERSUS SOCIAL AGGRESSION

To be able to communicate effectively police officers must be able to distinguish between two different states of aggression in the subject. These two states are **emotional** aggression and **social** aggression.

Football supporters walking along together chanting and gesticulating are likely to be displaying social aggression. They are acting as a group and behaving in a manner which they would not do individually. Using an empathetic problem-solving approach may annoy or simply irritate the group. An assertive approach on the other hand is likely to be respected and may gain some compliance from them.

People displaying social aggression will still be thinking rationally. Those behaving emotionally will be thinking irrationally.

The individual showing emotional aggression in a domestic situation may lash out if officers try an assertive approach, eg, 'Just pack it in! Sit down and be quiet!' An empathetic approach by the officers may calm the person down, eg by first stating their name and which police station they work at. This lets the person know that the officers are not faceless authority figures. Ask the person what has happened and offer to help. Asking open questions elicits more information than closed questions which invite 'yes' or 'no' answers. Listen intently to their problems. Often when people
'listen' they are really rehearsing mentally their next interruption. Summarise what they have said so that the problem becomes clear.

Being empathetic does not however mean that police officers act as 'doormats' or 'verbal punch bags' and allow the other person to violate the officers' rights as individuals. Remain flexible and have the ability to act assertively if the situation demands it.

THE EFFECTIVE COMMUNICATOR

To communicate effectively police officers need to possess certain qualities, namely:

I PERSONALITY – A friendly and confident style.

I MATURITY – To avoid acting in a way which would unintentionally upset or excite the individual.

I FLEXIBILITY – By listening intently to what others are saying and responding to their problems rather than imposing the officers own agenda on the situation.

I CAPABILITY – To be skilled as a 'verbal persuader'.

MANAGING ANGER

Anger is a natural emotion necessary to boost the fight or flight responses to dangerous situations. Anger can also be triggered by hurt, violation and frustration. In modern society people tend to view anger as a negative and potentially destructive force which must be controlled and bottled up. It is commonly thought that if people do not control their anger they will 'blow up' and act uncontrollably. Operational police officers must acknowledge that it is natural to experience anger. If, however, officers experience a highly stressed state, such as anger, for considerable periods of time their health will suffer. Some common problems associated with stress are:

I Heart disease and arterial damage.

I High blood pressure and raised cholesterol level.

I Digestive disorders.

There are other effects of stress which can wear officers down and even lead to depression. For the good of officers' health anger needs to be managed.

If officers allow their anger to be translated into aggression they can expect to meet resistance from the public and an increased likelihood of assault. To prevent officers' anger harming themselves or others a constructive approach is required. One such approach is known as 'assertive anger' (Lindenfield, 1993).

For example, officers attend a domestic dispute. There are no offences involved and after giving some advice they are walking away when one of those involved in the dispute says: 'That's right just get lost! I pay my taxes for you lot. You've done nothing like always.' The officers continue and the person follows them shouting, 'Why don't you try and catch the drug dealers and burglars around here? You're not welcome around here we can sort our own problems out. We don't need you'.

A couple of options are: to appear stoic and leave, or for the officers to express their feelings.

In order to express anger assertively individuals need to be **direct and specific**:

'I'm getting really annoyed by the comments you've made about me.
I happen to be a very hard working and conscientious officer.
I think it is really quite wrong to try and lay the blame for all criminal activity on me.
I would like you to think twice before making such comments.
I'm certain that with a little more co-operation around here the crime problem could be reduced.'

Notice the use of 'I' statements. The people whom the officers are addressing need to be receptive to these statements, or it will be a wasted exercise.

The danger with assertive language is that it can be perceived as aggressive language. Aggression is destructive, whereas assertiveness is used to express feelings and achieve a constructive outcome.

Stick to the present situation and do not try 'topic hopping' from one grievance to another.

It would only inflame the situation to respond aggressively, 'You're all the same here in Newtown.' Such a response fails to acknowledge the individuality of the person addressing the officer.

Do not try to moralise. If police officers 'tell' people what to do they will probably resent it and will very likely do the opposite of what the officers want.

ACTING ASSERTIVELY

What officers say is often as important as what they do.

The object of acting assertively is to make potential assailants comply with verbal commands. Make sure that these are easily understood and not open to misinterpretation.

Identification

It is normally wise for officers to announce that they are the police when approaching incidents. With the profusion of uniformed private security officers and the changes in police uniform, such as bomber jackets, officers may not be immediately recognised. This is especially important at night when trying to disperse a group of people who may be facing the other way and/or affected by alcohol. There will also be those who make mischief by assaulting officers and later, in court, claim that they did not know that it was a police officer they assaulted and therefore acted in 'self-defence'. If there is any room for doubt verbal commands should start with 'POLICE!' or 'POLICE OFFICER!' said sufficiently loudly for the individual and any potential witnesses to hear.

VERBAL COMMANDS

Verbal commands need to be **clear, concise** and issued by **one officer**.

▌ CLARITY – Commands should be given as simple instructions in plain English. The aim is for the subject to know that a command has been given and that if he disregards it his actions may be deemed as threatening behaviour. Being able to project the voice above the surrounding noise level is essential.

▌ BREVITY – Keep it simple. Commands must be short and sharp, not long winded and complex.

▌ ONE OFFICER – Too often several officers start barking out commands to an individual which are often contradictory, 'Don't move!' 'Get down on the floor!' 'Put your hands on the wall!' If only one officer issues the verbal commands confusion can be avoided.

The Construction of Verbal Commands

Verbal commands are usually constructed of three parts:

▌ IDENTIFICATION – To avoid misunderstanding start the verbal command with, 'Police!' if there is any chance that someone may not recognise the police officers as such.

▌ SIMPLE LAWFUL COMMAND – These commands are to preserve public safety. Examples are, 'Get back!' 'Standstill!' or 'Stop!' Avoid giving commands which can seem like a challenge to the individual, eg, 'Don't swing that baseball bat at me!' Some people may be prompted to do the opposite of what the officer wants them to do. Commands should therefore not contain, 'Don't ...'.

▌ EXTENSION OF LAWFUL COMMAND – These commands direct the behaviour of the individual to ensure public safety. Examples are, 'Move back!' 'Show me your hands!' 'Put your arms straight up!' 'Turn around!'.

For example:
An arrest has taken place and the subject is being restrained on the

Use verbal commands to keep the bystander away.

Consider other reasonable force options if commands are ignored.

ground by officers. An officer is providing cover to protect the scene. A second person walks over towards the group shouting, 'You're out of order. Get off him!'

The officer uses the following verbal command, 'POLICE! STAND STILL!'

If the person complies with the command order him to, 'Move back!' and then explain what is happening and advise him to keep away. If he disobeys the command and keeps on advancing consider drawing the baton to defend and give a further command, 'STAND STILL!', 'GET BACK!' or simply 'BACK!'. Emphasis can be added to the commands by saying, 'Do it now!'. If justified and the subject continues to advance, consider a baton technique for protection. At this stage the person concerned has used aggressive language and has disobeyed at least two verbal commands to stand still. If the subject continues to advance it does not take a genius to assume that his intentions are hostile.

Use verbal commands whenever engaging an individual with a search technique or an arrest technique. This ensures that the person knows what is wanted of him or her. It also gives an indication of whether the person is compliant or not. Officers maintain the initiative by constantly talking the person through what he has to do, what the officers are doing and the reasons for their actions.

GOWISE acronym for section 1 PACE stop and search:

State the **grounds** for the search.
State the **object** of the search.
Show **warrant** card (if in plain clothes).
Officer **identifies** himself or herself.
Officer says which police **station** he or she is attached to.
Subject informed of the **entitlement** to a copy of the search record.

'Turn round and face the wall. Now'
'Put both arms straight up. Now'
'Lock your elbows out...'.

Keep a constant stream of commands, questions and explanations going to dominate the situation. If the person hesitates repeat the command and say, 'Do it now'. If individuals are allowed to get the upper hand verbally by officers leaving pauses, they may exploit it and distract the officers from the search.

ASSERTIVE TECHNIQUES

Broken Record

A useful assertive technique is 'Broken Record'.

Where a subject is trying to get the better of officers in a verbal exchange do not let him or her get away from the point being made. This approach is in contrast to empathy where officers are flexible and respond to what the individual wants to talk about.

Take a situation where officers are trying to use assertiveness to get an argumentative person out of a house. Once they have been requested to leave by the house owner and have refused to go the officers mentally prepare their broken record, namely, 'Leave the house now.'

A verbal interchange may go something like this:

I *Officer:* 'You've been told to go by your ex-girlfriend so **leave the house now.**'

I *Subject:* 'But I haven't finished trying to patch things up between us.'

I *Officer:* 'You'll have to do that another day. **Leave the house now.**'

I *Subject:* 'Where am I going to stay tonight then?'

I *Officer:* 'We can discuss that outside if you **leave the house now.**'

Every time the subject tries to change the topic bring them back and repeat the 'broken record'. Broken record is intended simply to wear out the subject until he or she realises the futility of further argument and complies with the request. It takes little mental effort on the part of the officer to continue this provided it does not turn the argumentative subject into an aggressive subject.

Observant officers can detect when individuals are becoming agitated by being sensitive. Any of these cues, either on their own or combined with others, may indicate that the subject is becoming aggressive:

▎ Breathing becomes rapid and shallow.

▎ Eyes are wide open and the pupils are dilated. Subjects may try to 'out stare' the officer.

▎ Face may change colour going paler or redder.

▎ Voice may change to louder, higher and quicker. Alternatively the change may be to a soft and deliberate tone.

▎ Ritualistic language which may indicate what the subject intends to do, 'You want to punch my lights out officer. Don't you? That's what you want to do. Yeah. Punch my lights out'. What the subject is really saying is that is what he or she actually wants to do to the officer.

▎ The head tilts back and the subject stands tall.

▎ Large movements of the arms, including finger pointing.

Basically any change in the behaviour of the person concerned should immediately cause officers to increase their state of awareness. Watch for inconsistent behaviour, ie, the noisy person who suddenly becomes quiet.

If the individual is not calmed down he or she may attack the police officer. The officer may detect some of the following danger cues before the individual launches an attack.

▎ Abusive language.

▎ The individual stops staring to depersonalise the officer. His eyes may glance at an intended target for attack.

▎ The muscles tense in the face and the fists clench. The hands are held above waist height.

▎ The body lowers immediately before rushing forwards to attack.

▎ The subject moves forwards reducing the reactionary gap.

Defusing Tense Individuals

Officers should be skilled at reducing tension in others to prevent them launching an attack. Each officer will have his or her own techniques, here are some methods of reducing tension:

I Keep out of the other person's personal space and do not stand directly in front of him.

I Adopt the open stance and use active listening skills.

I Remove the individual from an audience, or the audience from the individual.

I Talk softly to the subject and show him or her respect.

I Remain calm by deep breathing.

Fogging

Another useful assertive technique to take the wind out of an argumentative subject's sails is called 'fogging'. Police officers can use this to deal with the substance of a subject's argument by agreeing with them and then moving the conversation on to the point the officer wants to make. Once the subject has no argument left officers can use assertive language to obtain compliance to their request.

I *Subject:* 'This is just typical. You police officers have a very bad attitude. You're always victimising us.'

I *Officer:* 'There's truth in what you say. If there are people in society with bad attitudes then there will unfortunately be police officers with bad attitudes. Now move your vehicle.'

Basically, the person can **say what he wants** providing he **does what you want**.

EMPLOYING EMPATHY

Empathy can be described as a 'feeling for, or a capacity for, sharing in the interests of another'. As well as empathy, police officers must be able to adopt a problem-solving approach which includes bargaining and compromise.

The basic principles of the empathetic approach are:

I INTEGRITY – Be totally honest with the person.

I RESPECT – Preserve the self-esteem of the individual.

I APPEAL – Appeal to the rational side of the subject, request that he act reasonably.

Guidelines

To communicate with empathy consider the following guidelines which will help to establish a rapport:

Basic Ground Rules
Develop an honest atmosphere and avoid pretence and arrogance. Project an image of integrity.
First impressions count. Do not excite the other person by sudden movements.
Show a willingness to resolve the problem by peaceful means and co-operation.

What officers should know:

I REASON – Why has this person ended up in this situation at this time and under these circumstances?

I CAUSE – What is the root cause of the problem from his perspective?

I PRIORITISE – Which problem must be dealt with first before other problems can be handled?

I RESOURCES – What resources are available to the officer and to the subject?

The longer the verbal interchange can be maintained the greater the likelihood of a positive outcome – **the time factor**.

Introduction
Police officers must introduce themselves to the subject, telling the sub-ject their name, where they work and the fact that they are willing to help. Obtain the person's name and use it to gain increased interest by personalising the interchange.

Atmosphere
The aim is to create an atmosphere between the individual and the offi-cer which will allow the development of a positive emotional attitude by transfer from the officer to the subject.

Methods by which such a transference may be developed:

I Be viewed as a real person.

I Use an attitude which is objective and non-judgmental.

I Convey calmness and control – the other person is more anxious and vulnerable than the officer.

I Exude warmth and empathy.

I Build trust with the individual.

I Ask for co-operation.

I Do not make promises which cannot be kept.

Active Listening

Pay attention to what is being said.

Listen for any indications of an emotional state and for any changes in mood.

Officers should let the person know that they are listening and interested by giving positive NVCs, eg, a nod or a smile.

Communicating

Avoid lecturing, moralising, or giving advice.

Carefully select the words, tone and manner. Speak slowly and softly.

Get the subject to participate. Ask open questions, ie, what? where? who? why? when? and how?

Pitch the conversation at the other person's educational and vocabulary level. Be positive.

Clarify what the individual is saying and check the meaning with him or her by summarising what has been said.

Remember the value of silence. Pauses can be used to advantage. They provide time to think and prompt the other person to fill the vacuum of silence.

A very useful acronym is LEAP:

LISTEN actively

EMPATHISE with the other person

ASK open questions

PARAPHRASE what has been said.

Problem Solving

Try and keep the individual in a problem-solving frame of mind.

Police officers must 'invest' their resources in the encounter. If officers can reduce the tension in the subject, he or she will return to a normal functioning level and resume thinking rationally.

Seek a detailed explanation of the person's current problem. Be aware that the incident which caused the crisis may well have been violent and the individual may well not want to dwell on it. In some cases (especially potential suicides) an event may have occurred recently which has been beyond the individual's normal coping mechanism.

COMMUNICATING WITH THE AWKWARD CUSTOMER

The late Robert Kennedy once said, 'One fifth of the people are against everything all the time'. Many people that officers talk to fit into this category. Police officers are criticised for not catching criminals by the same people who object to the police patrolling their neighbourhood. Officers can end up feeling that they just cannot please some people. George Thompson, the author of *Verbal Judo*, recommends using the Five Step Hard Style to communicate with awkward people. This method is 'street proven' as Mr Thompson was a police officer for many years.

The Five Step Hard Style is:

▌ ASK – Officers make an appeal for the person to do what they want him to do.

▌ SET CONTEXT – Officers then explain the reason why they are making the request.

▌ DETAIL OPTIONS – Officers specifically detail what will happen if the person does or does not comply.

▌ CONFIRM – The officers give the person the power to make his choice of the options.

▌ ACT – Finally the officers take appropriate action. This could be an arrest or a search, whatever they are lawfully entitled to do.

Example of the Five Step Hard Style in action:

A police officer stops a vehicle for speeding and finds that there is no current keeper details on the PNC. The driver cannot produce his driving licence and the officer requests his details, but he steadfastly refuses to give his date of birth which is a summary offence.

▌ ASK – 'Please tell me your correct date of birth.'

▌ CONTEXT – 'As you can't produce a driver's licence now I need to know your date of birth so I can make a check to see if you are disqualified or wanted.'

▌ OPTIONS – 'If I can check you are not wanted you can go on your way tonight. You will be able to sit at home with your family in front of your telly and put your feet up or go down the pub with your friends. If you do not give me your date of birth then I can't confirm who you are. In which case you will end up staying with us in a cell at the police station until we can sort out exactly who you are.'

▌ CONFIRM – 'Now is there anything I can say or do to obtain your co-operation? I really hope there is.'

▌ ACT – If the officer has reached this stage without compliance he or she needs to look at what legal options are left. The officer may be justified in arresting the individual at this stage. He has been given every chance to co-operate. If there are two officers involved who are familiar with this five step style then they will know that a negative response to step four, 'confirm', will be their cue to act simultaneously.

It is important for officers not to loose their temper with awkward people. Be very specific about the options of their going home or going to the cells. Allow them the power to choose the option of compliance or arrest. Do not force them into a stand off, 'Give me your date of birth or I'll lock you up!' They will probably not want to back down from this challenge.

SUMMARY

Communication skills are every bit as important as physical contact skills to protect police officers. Officers can reflect on their verbal interchanges and consider:

I What approaches could I have used? Assertive or empathetic.

I Was the approach I took the most appropriate one in the circumstances?

I In what ways could I have improved my communication with the subject?

With time and effort officers will become proficient in the other four Street Survival Skills, but communication skills will take the rest of their lives to master.

Recommended Reading

George J Thompson PhD and Jerry B Jenkins (1993) *Verbal Judo. The Gentle Art of Persuasion*, William Morrow & Co, New York

Rolland Ouellette (1993) *Management of Aggressive Behaviour*, Performance Dimensions Publishing, Powers Lake, Wisconsin.

Chapter six

THE USE OF FORCE

KEYPOINTS

Use this chapter to find out:

I *What is the conflict resolution model.*

I *How to justify the use of force in writing.*

Chapter six

The Use of Force

Police officers are accountable to the criminal and civil law; the discipline code; and their own consciences. In our society the police have virtually monopolised the use of lawful force. Force can only be used when it is justifiable and officers must therefore be confident that they know what common and statute law governs the police use of force, namely:

▌ Self-defence.

▌ Breach of the peace.

▌ Saving life.

▌ Police and Criminal Evidence Act 1984, section 117.

▌ Criminal Law Act 1967, section 3.

   In addition to the legislation listed above, police officers need to know in what circumstances reasonable force can be used. They also need to be able to articulate the reasons for using force, either in writing or when giving oral evidence. This chapter will cover the conflict resolution model and the use of force reporting.

CONFLICT RESOLUTION MODEL

In an attempt to give some practical guidance on when 'reasonable force' can be used, a hypothetical model has been created by police forces and training organisations called the conflict resolution model.

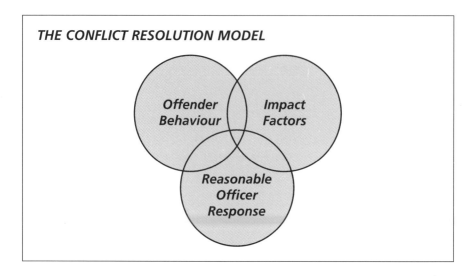

THE CONFLICT RESOLUTION MODEL

Offender Behaviour

Impact Factors

Reasonable Officer Response

The thinking behind the model is simple. A reasonable officer's response to resolving a conflict will depend upon the behaviour of the subject and any factors which impact on the situation.

Subject Behaviour

The behaviour of the subject determines the level of force a reasonable officer will use. The behaviour will fall into one of the following profiles:

▍ COMPLIANCE.
  The subject follows the commands of the officer.

▍ RESISTANCE – verbal and non-verbal.
  Danger cues, both verbal and non-verbal.

▍ RESISTANCE – passive.
  Non-compliance to lawful police commands.
  Refusal to move.

▍ RESISTANCE – active.
  Physical resistance to police officer by pulling and pushing.

▍ RESISTANCE – assaultive.
  Wrestling with the police officer, headbutting, punching and kicking.

▍ RESISTANCE – aggravated.
  Serious assault on the police officer.
  Use, or attempted use, of weapons.

Impact Factors

The impact factors work both ways. A police officer may be confronted by an aggressive person of average height and build. If the officer is smaller, weaker and fatigued it may be reasonable to use a certain amount of force. That same amount of force may not be reasonable if the officer is bigger, stronger and fitter than the aggressive person.

The impact factors can be anything which is relevant to the subject and the police officer and affects the use of force decision-making process.

Motivation
  Drunk – Excessive alcohol consumption.
  Drugged – Substance misuse (drugs or solvents).
  Desperate – Reckless actions to avoid arrest.
  Disturbed – Mentally disordered or emotionally angry.

Opportunity
  Access to weapons.
  Proximity of the subject to the officer, imminent danger.
  Position of advantage, eg, officer on the ground.

The number of people present.
The subject has the advantage of surprise.

Capability
Age.
Gender.
Build (height and weight) relative to the officer.
Ability, or apparent ability, in combative skills, such as boxing or martial arts.
Warning signals, if known.
Knowledge of antecedents (criminal history) or previous encounters with the subject.
Ailments, particularly contagious diseases.

This list of impact factors is not definitive. An impact factor could be literally anything which impacts upon the use of force decision. A police officer may be able to justify the use of a certain technique to control a subject quickly using two impact factors. Firstly, the subject was believed to be infected with a serious contagious disease which could have been transmitted to the officer had the incident resulted in the officer wrestling with the subject. Secondly, the officer had an old back injury which could have been aggravated by physically grappling with the subject.

Reasonable Officer's Response

The officer will assess the subject's behaviour and the impact factors before choosing one of the following reasonable options:

I Physical presence.

I Communication skills.
Tactical communications, including the five step style.
Verbal commands, lawful orders.

I Primary control skills.
The escort hold.

I Secondary control skills.
Incapacitant spray.

I Defensive tactics.
Empty-hand techniques.
Baton techniques.

I Deadly force.

The use of force is not an exact science. In *Reed v Wastle* even the courts realised this, 'In the circumstances one did not use jewellers scales to measure reasonable force'. Whether an officer's actions were 'reasonable' or not would depend entirely on the circumstances.

The reasonable officer will choose the appropriate option bearing in mind the subject's behaviour and impact factors. This decision needs to be committed to paper in the form of original notes or a witness statement for it to withstand scrutiny afterwards.

PRACTICAL USE OF FORCE

The vast majority of searches and arrests are done without any resistance. There are occasions however where police officers have to resort to force. In the case of an aggressive potential assailant an officer would use force to effect an arrest. A defendant would be able to avoid being found guilty of 'police assault' if he or she could prove that the officer was not acting in the 'lawful execution of your duty'. Although not in the scope of this book, police officers should nevertheless be sure in their own minds that they can answer the following questions:

❙ What has the person done?

❙ Does this constitute an offence?

❙ Is there a power to arrest for this offence?

❙ Are there sufficient grounds for making an arrest?

In most cases the facts speak for themselves and it is more than obvious that the person can, and should, be arrested. Police officers will need to describe **in detail** the circumstances which led them to use force in original notes and statements. Officers may be called to justify their actions months or even years later at criminal, civil or disciplinary hearings. Some training has tended to concentrate on the physical skills of using batons and handcuffs at the expense of the knowledge of the circumstances which justify their use. Officers' accounts of the use of force are similar to painting by numbers; if gaps are left out of the picture who is going to fill them in? At a hearing others may try to fill in the gaps officers have left in their testimony which may, or may not, be correct. Ensure that a full and accurate picture is painted by covering all relevant factors concerning the use of force as well as the evidence of the offence. Officers will need to rely on the accounts they made at the time to assist them at a later date. If officers describe an encounter in the following terms they leave a lot of questions unanswered:

'At 01.45 hours on Sunday the 21st of April 19XX I attended outside Wolfie's Night Club, Main Street, Anytown, where I saw a man who I now know to be the defendant, Alan Jenkins. As a result of what I was told by the Manager of the night club, Peter Green, I approached the defendant.

I said to the defendant, 'You are under arrest for assaulting a member of the door staff at Wolfie's night club,' and I cautioned him to which he made no reply.

I took hold of his arm and escorted him to a police vehicle. The defendant became abusive and resisted. A struggle took place during which I used my baton and the defendant ended up on the pavement. I placed the defendant in handcuffs and transported him to the Police Station.

The following questions may require detailed answers at a future hearing into why force was used.

Attendance

▮ Were you in uniform or plain clothes?

▮ Was there any chance that the defendant did not know you were a police officer?

▮ If you were in plain clothes did you display your warrant card?

▮ What type of vehicle did you arrive in?

▮ Was it a marked saloon vehicle or personnel carrier?

Approach

▮ When you first saw the defendant what did you observe?

▮ From your observations what assessment did you make?

▮ What communication took place between you and the defendant?

▮ What commands did you give?

Relevant Factors

Impacting on the Subject

▮ What was the seriousness of the offence alleged?

▮ What was motivating the defendant to escape from arrest?

▮ What influences were affecting the subject?
(Alcohol, drugs, solvents, mental disorder or emotional anger.)

▮ What was the distance between the defendant and yourself?

▮ What weapons were available to the defendant?

▮ Did the defendant have the benefit of surprise?

▮ What was the capability of the defendant?
(Age, gender, build (relative to you), combative ability, warning signals known, antecedents or ailments.)

Impacting on the Environment

I Were there any associates of the defendant nearby?

I Were there any bystanders who have might intervened to assist the defendant?

I Were there any objects nearby which could have been used as weapons?

Impacting upon your Own Resources

I How many police officers were available to assist you?

I Were any specialist officers available to back you up?

I What was your capability ? (Age, gender, build, fitness and skill.)

I How fatigued were you?

I What protective equipment did you have?

I How much time did you have available to deal with this incident?

I Did you have the element of surprise?

Defendant's Behaviour

I What did the defendant do by actions or words which implied:
Threats?
Aggression?
Resistance?

I What response did the defendant make to your verbal commands and actions?

Your Actions

I Exactly what control methods did you use?
(Drawing of handcuffs or baton, use of equipment, eg, tactical handcuffing and/or baton techniques.)

I What injuries were caused to anyone?

I What steps did you take to calm down the situation?

Escort

I How suitable was the vehicle for transporting a violent prisoner?

I What was the distance between the point of arrest and the police station?

I How long would this have normally taken?

I What was the defendant's behaviour whilst being transported?

I Did the defendant continue to resist whilst being transported?

To include all this information in original notes and statements may seem like a very tall order but if officers are to survive not only the street, but also later in court, they must be able to articulate exactly why force was used. Appendix 1 is an example of an arrest statement and attempts to include a more detailed justification for the arrest and use of force outside Wolfie's night club. Legal purists will highlight the inadmissible hearsay in the statement. Even if some parts are not read out at court they will support the officer's judgement for the use of force.

Appendix 1 is not meant to be an example of best practice where officer safety is concerned. The reason for including it is to illustrate the amount of detail which may well be required to justify the use of force. If officers normally write a minimum of detail in their statements they will find it difficult, if not impossible, to recall the factors which led them to use force at a hearing in several months time.

The public are witnessing the use by police of new equipment which at first may appear unreasonable and the basis for a complaint. By detailed accounts in notes and statements officers will justify their proper use of force. Many senior police officers will not have undergone baton or rigid handcuff training and the detailed account which officers provide will explain the reasoning behind their actions.

SUMMARY

When faced with potential assailants who have the motivation, opportunity or capability to cause injury officers must succeed in restraining them. Coming off second best may mean being seriously injured, or worse.

The decision to escalate a situation lies with the subject. If the potential assailant takes the decision to escalate the confrontation that is his choice. Police officers must be ready to use force to protect themselves and to restrain the would be attacker. Section 3 of the Criminal Law Act 1967 governs police officers' conduct; the criminals have no rule book.

Finally, officers should present a detailed account of the circumstances to demonstrate that their actions were 'reasonable'.

Chapter seven

SEARCH SKILLS

KEYPOINTS

Use this chapter to find out:

I *What legislation governs searches.*

I *What are the guidelines for searching.*

I *How to conduct searches safely and effectively.*

Chapter seven

Search Skills

When police officers search suspects they reduce the distance between them from a safe reactionary gap to close quarters. As most injuries are inflicted on officers by punches, kicks and headbutts it is obvious that it is more dangerous the closer officers get to the subjects. Each approach to a suspect must be the safest possible in the circumstances.

SEARCH TECHNIQUES

Conducting searches is an integral part of operational policing and officers should aim at being masters of searching safely and thoroughly.

The risk of being assaulted whilst conducting a search is high for the following reasons:

▌ By necessity officers have lost the protection of a reactionary gap and they may become distracted by the search process at the expense of their own safety.

▌ Like effecting an arrest, the search is a 'flashpoint' where individuals may well assault officers in an attempt to avoid being arrested.

▌ Criminals may use articles on them, such as screwdrivers, to inflict injury.

An added danger when searching is the risk of infection caused by puncture wounds from sharp objects.

EXTENT OF SEARCHES

Strip searches and intimate searches are governed by the Police and Criminal Evidence Act 1984 and are normally conducted at a police station. This chapter will concentrate on those searches conducted on the street, the 'frisk' and the 'thorough'. The 'frisk' search is the minimum search required to detect a hidden weapon, such as a small knife. A 'thorough' search is intended to uncover smaller items, like a drugs wrap.

The extent of the search will depend upon the circumstances taking into consideration such factors as:

▌ WHERE? – The location of the search. Is it in public view?

▌ WHAT? – What article(s) are being searched for?

▌ WHY? – What powers are being used to conduct the search? Is the search necessary?

▌ WHO? – The gender of the person and the officer.

LEGISLATION

A good working knowledge of the law relating to searches is essential when dealing with the public. Knowledge of the following legislation is a must for the operational police officer:

▎ Section 1, Police and Criminal Evidence Act 1984 –
gives power to stop and search persons and vehicles for stolen goods or prohibited articles.

▎ The PACE Codes of Practice –
give guidelines relating to 'reasonable suspicion'.

▎ Section 23(2), Misuse of Drugs Act 1971 –
gives power to stop and search persons and vehicles for controlled drugs.

▎ Section 32(1), Police and Criminal Evidence Act 1984 –
gives power to search persons after arrest.

▎ Section 53(1), Police and Criminal Evidence Act 1984 –
gives power to search detainees in custody and for intimate searches.

USE OF FORCE IN CONDUCTING SEARCHES

People may be apprehensive about being searched whether or not they have incriminating articles on them. Explaining the grounds for the search can reduce tension and prevent hostility. This explanation should enable the search to be conducted in a professional manner.

In PACE-related searches police officers may use reasonable force under section 117, Police and Criminal Evidence Act 1984. If a person obstructs a lawful search he commits an offence under section 51, Police Act 1964. In high risk searches where officers have reasonable cause to suspect that the subject is in possession of a weapon they may consider the use of handcuffs. Handcuffs are not solely used on persons who have been arrested, but can be used in the course of exercising a power to search **if the circumstances justify it**.

There is a specific offence of obstruction in relation to drug searches, namely section 23(4), Misuse of Drugs Act 1971.

SEARCH PROCEDURE

Before searching police officers will have needed to assess the situation and to have communicated with the subject.

Assess:

▎ OBJECTIVE – Officers need to be clear about the object of the search. Is it for stolen goods, weapons or drugs? What legislation and police powers are involved?

I SUBJECT – Officers need to examine the individual visually for any danger cues, hidden weapons, signs of drink or drugs, etc.

I ENVIRONMENT – Do the surroundings allow the officer to control the search? If not can the individual be directed to a better location for the search or is it practical to carry out the search in a van?

I OWN RESOURCES – Are there sufficient officers to conduct the search safely and cover the searching officer?

I OPTIONS – Having assessed the situation and reviewed the options the officer decides to proceed and conduct a search.

Communicate

Good communication is essential for an effective search so control the search by verbal commands. If officers' verbal skills are poor the subject will be allowed to influence the conduct of the search and it is likely to be fruitless. Develop an almost prepared mental script to assist in controlling the search.

When officers communicate they will be in the interview position, ie, ten o'clock or two o'clock. If the individual turns to face the officer straight on, or moves towards him or her, the officer should tell the person, 'Stand still'. Explain that it is for everyone's safety that the instructions are followed. Adopt the interview stance and have a colleague in a cover position. Explain the grounds and object of the search using the GOWISE mnemonic.

I GROUNDS – State the grounds for the search.

I OBJECT – State the object of the search.

Before searching consider stance, reactionary gap and environment.

▌ WARRANT – Show your warrant card if in plain clothes.

▌ IDENTIFICATION – State who you are.

▌ STATION – State the police station you work from.

▌ ENTITLEMENT – Inform the individual that he is entitled to a written record of the search for a period of 12 months after the search.

Officers should think carefully about what they are going to say. Talk deliberately and use an appropriate tone to convey the message of control.

Before officers move into close quarters to effect the search they need to know whether or not the person complies with their instructions and whether or not there are likely to be any hidden weapons.

One script officers may consider employing is:

'Do you have any weapons, drugs, stolen goods or anything else you shouldn't have on you?'

'Put both your arms straight up.'

'Keep your arms straight out. Lock out your elbows.'

'Open you hands and spread your fingers.'

'Turn around slowly to face away from me.'

Give each instruction as a command and do not rush. When the subject complies with a command give the next one. Visually examine the individual as he turns around. This is called the 'visual frisk'. Any unnatural bulges will be easier to see if the person's arms are raised, out to the side or straight up, as the clothing is pulled tighter.

Visually search the individual.

Watch out for the individuals who make a 'security pat'. They may touch a concealed weapon to reassure themselves that it is still hidden or they may turn their bodies so that their weapon side is away from the officer.

Only if individuals have complied with the instructions should officers proceed with the search.

GENERAL GUIDELINES FOR SEARCHES

Generally male officers should search males and female officers should search females. There are occasions when this is not possible. If police officers have to search a member of the opposite sex they should get it witnessed by another officer or even a civilian. Record the personal details of any witnesses should any accusations be made.

Stabilise the individual with one hand and search with the other. Officers should pat and squeeze clothing, rather than sliding their hands along, when searching.

Ensure that the search is done thoroughly by overlapping the search. Think about conducting the search twice; the first time around will be a preliminary frisk search for safety reasons to detect any weapons; the second time will be slower and more systematic search for smaller items.

Readers need to be aware of their powers when searching persons under section 1 PACE (stop and search). The search will be limited to that necessary to satisfy the object of the search. Officers will find it difficult, if not impossible, to justify overlapping search areas or searching a person twice using PACE stop and search powers.

Do not search without controlling the person physically. The individual should either be in handcuffs or controlled by holding on to one of his wrists or fingers. Keep the person slightly off balance.

Make sure the individual does not have anything in the palms of his hands.

Keep talking to the individual, giving him instructions or asking him questions. Ask him if he has anything on him that could cause harm or if he injects drugs. Reduce his tension by asking him if he has any, 'Kalashnikovs, Semtex,...'.

Be flexible and prepared to adapt the search technique to the circumstances.

Never assume that a search is just 'routine'. Keep thinking at all times and search thoroughly.

Before searching each pocket ask the person to describe what should be in the pocket. Gently squeeze the pocket from the outside. Consider wearing gloves and using a search stick or pen to prevent injury.

Thoroughly search the 'hot spots' for hidden weapons: waistband area, crotch, all pockets, hands, wrists and ankles, clothing, footwear and bags.

If individuals are permitted to remove the contents of their pockets they could suddenly pull out a weapon even if an officer is holding their forearm.

If the contents of the pockets are harmless, eg, a wallet or personal papers, instruct the subjects to keep them in their hands rather than replace them in their pockets, they may be less inclined to attack with their hands full of their own property.

When officers make a 'find' they should announce it to their colleagues by saying what the item is and where it was found, eg, 'Screwdriver in rear right trouser pocket'. Place any find which is evidential or could be used as a weapon in a safe place. If officers find used unprotected needles it will be safer to push the points into the ground rather than in their pockets.

Always suspect that there are more 'finds' on the subject. Use the 'plus one' rule, eg, if one knife is found on the person look for another one. (Remember the limitations imposed by section 1 of PACE.)

Do not mentally limit the search. For example if the search is for stolen goods also think, 'weapons!'. After all police officers are paid to be suspicious.

A sheathed knife can be tucked into the officer's waistband. Unprotected knives can be slid between a pouch and the officer's belt.

SEARCH METHODS

The search method chosen will be down to personal preference and the circumstances. The following are methods of searching which may be considered. Police officers can only use these searches where compliance has been gained. In other words, the person has done as instructed and has turned to face away from the officer with his arms up or out to the sides.

Whichever search method is used, stand behind the person at the 6 o'clock position and have physical control of one or ideally both of his hands.

Professional officers must overcome their own embarrassment when searching the intimate parts of individuals of the same sex. Criminals often 'crotch' weapons which they have subsequently used on police officers. If officers fail to search these areas they could literally die of embarrassment.

First Method – Arms Outstretched

The officer moves cautiously in behind the male and takes hold of his wrist. With his free hand the officer searches the front systematically keeping the male's other hand in sight at all times.

The officer holds the subject's wrist whilst searching, in a systematic manner, with the other hand.

The officer searches from the other side remembering to overlap the searched areas.

The officer keeps talking to the male all the time. After searching one side front and rear the officer moves over and grips the male's other wrist and continues the search.

The officer maintains physical control over the subject by holding one of his wrists in a loose wrist lock. If the officer meets resistance he can control the subject by applying pressure to the wrist; also, by holding one of the wrists, he is given early warning of any hostile action by the male. If resistance is encountered the officer could use a wrist lock and verbal commands. If this does not control the subject the officer could consider using other defensive tactics to stun the subject and regain control.

The subject could be placed slightly off balance if the officer instructs the subject to point his toes inwards and lean back towards the officer. The subject's free hand could be more easily observed if it is placed on the subject's head.

The next search method is safer as the officer controls both of the subject's hands.

Second Method – Hands behind Back

Instruct the subject.

'Put your hands behind your back.'

'Move your feet further apart.'

'Turn your toes in.' (This places the person in an awkward position if he wants to attack the officer as he will have to move his feet first which should be the officer's cue that something is wrong.)

The officer moves in behind the male and takes physical control of both his hands. The beauty of this method is that it does not matter if the hands are palm to palm, back to back or fingers interlocked, the officer can still control both hands in one of his.

As in the last search technique, the officer searches the male systematically, changing hands when necessary.

Third Method – Hands on Head

This method is similar to the one above. The officer instructs the subject to put his hands on top of his head and interlock his fingers. The officer moves in behind the subject and controls both of his hands.

If serious resistance is encountered during the search, the officer can attempt to control the individual by applying pressure to the hands and using verbal commands.

THE UNCO-OPERATIVE SUBJECT

There will be some people who will not comply with a police officer's instructions or will walk away. Either they have something to hide or are being deliberately awkward.

Officers will not be privy to what these people are thinking, or the reasons why they are being unco-operative. Re-assess the situation and look at what options are available.

▎ Is there sufficient reasonable suspicion to justify arrest?

▎ If 'Yes' – Consider applying a restraint technique and arrest.

▎ If 'No' – Is there sufficient reasonable suspicion to justify continuing to use powers to stop and search without consent?

▎ If 'Yes' – Consider restraining the person and applying handcuffs if the circumstances justify their use before searching.

▎ If 'No' - Can you persuade the person to co-operate by communication. 'Work with me. We are having a lot of burglaries in this area. I'm sure you want to help. Just co-operate for a couple of minutes.'

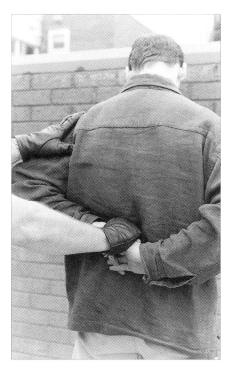

Above left: Fingers interlocked.

Above right: Hands back to back.

Right: Hands palm to palm.

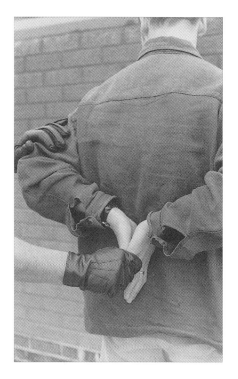

▌ If 'Yes' – Proceed with the search. Exercise even greater caution. Why was the person unco-operative? What has he/she got to hide?

▌ If 'No' – Say good-bye.

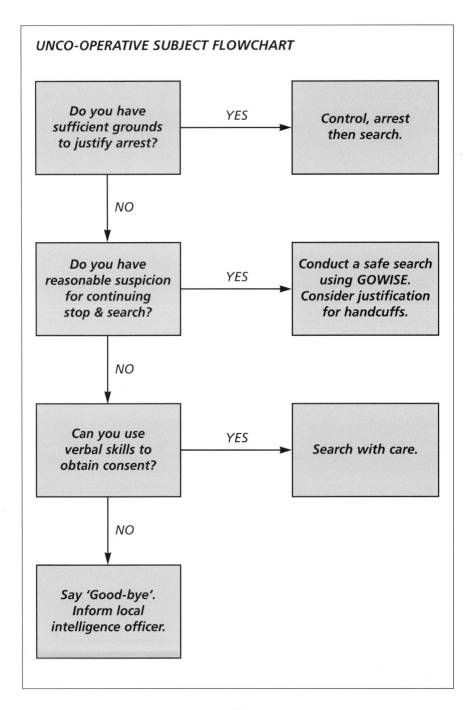

UNCO-OPERATIVE SUBJECT FLOWCHART

Do you have sufficient grounds to justify arrest?
→ *YES* → **Control, arrest then search.**

NO ↓

Do you have reasonable suspicion for continuing stop & search?
→ *YES* → **Conduct a safe search using GOWISE. Consider justification for handcuffs.**

NO ↓

Can you use verbal skills to obtain consent?
→ *YES* → **Search with care.**

NO ↓

Say 'Good-bye'. Inform local intelligence officer.

HIGH RISK SEARCHES

The high risk search techniques are for those people who pose a substantial risk of causing serious injury. An individual fitting the description of an offender who recently robbed another person at knifepoint would be an example of someone who poses a substantial risk of serious injury to the public, although there may be insufficient grounds to justify an immediate arrest. If a firearm was believed to have been involved summon armed police assistance.

The objective of the high risk search is public safety. Consider the safety of police officers and any bystanders.

Principles of the High Risk Search

The same stop and search principles apply, namely:

▌ Control the verbal interchange. Give clear instructions in an assertive manner.

▌ Maintain a safe distance.

▌ Use the contact and cover tactic.

▌ Consider drawing the baton for protection.

High Risk – Kneeling Search

As with the stop and search instruct the individual to:

▌ Raise his arms straight up.

▌ Open his hands and spread his fingers.

▌ Get him to turn slowly around so that he faces away from the searcher.

Then tell him to slowly drop down onto his knees. Place his hands on top of his head with his fingers interlocked and cross his ankles.

The officer tells the male, 'Don't move'. The officer then rings his baton and draws his handcuffs. Quietly the officer moves in behind the person and secures his hands with handcuffs to the rear, if the use of handcuffs can be justified.

For additional safety the officer can instruct the male to cross his ankles and the officer can then lightly rest his foot on the ankles.

High Risk – Prone Search

The high risk prone search procedure is very similar to the one described above. However instead of the person facing away from the officer, the officer instructs him to slowly turn right around and return to him.

The officer instructs the subject to interlock his fingers on top of his head in this high risk search.

The officer systematically searches the male once he has been controlled.

The officer gets the male to kneel down and then to lie down on his front with his arms straight out. When he is lying face down the officer instructs him to put his arms straight out to the sides and place his palms up. The male can be instructed to move his feet apart and place his ankles on the floor or simply to cross his legs.

The officer then rings his baton and draws his handcuffs. The male is told, 'Don't move', as the officer quietly moves in on the person's blind side, and handcuffs to the rear. The handcuffs are checked for tightness and double locked.

The officer keeps talking to the male to inform him of what he is doing and keeps the subject's hands off his back until he has searched the rear waistband area and rear pockets which could conceal a weapon.

The officer assesses the condition of the male. If the subject is over-weight, ill, intoxicated, or has recently exerted himself he has a risk of asphyxia due to the posture he is in. If his breathing becomes laboured or he complains of difficulty in breathing the officer must get him into a seated position quickly.

The high risk prone search should be done with at least two officers.

When handcuffing the subject the officer must monitor the subject for signs of breathing difficulties.

Once the search is complete, the officer rolls the person onto his side and sits him up. When the officer is ready to stand the person up, he instructs him to bend one of his knees and tells the subject that he is going to help him up by pushing him towards his bent knee.

Searching on Arrest

Under section 32 of PACE police officers have the power to search an arrested person where he 'may present a danger to himself or others', or have articles for use in an escape or evidence. If a person has been handcuffed before being brought into a police station search him before removing the handcuffs.

SEARCHING IN A POLICE STATION

Sections 54 and 55 of PACE give powers for properly authorised strip or intimate searches.

A thorough search should be made of arrested persons when they are received into custody on the instruction of the custody officer. It is not

The officer assists the subject to his feet.

uncommon for searches of police cells to reveal stolen goods and weapons secreted by detainees. It is therefore wise to check cells before detainees are placed into them and conduct a search of the detainees as they leave the cells.

SUMMARY

Searching should not be undertaken lightly or on a whim. The ground and object for each search should be clear.

Assess the dangers and use the most appropriate search technique such as:

I STANDING – Arms outstretched.

I STANDING – Hands behind back.

I STANDING – Hands on head.

I HIGH RISK – Kneeling.

I HIGH RISK – Prone.

Adopt a flexible approach and explain what is happening to bystanders as well as to the individual, if circumstances permit.

ARREST SKILLS

KEYPOINTS

Use this chapter to find out:

I *How to tackle people who physically resist when arrested.*

I *How to deal with resistance to the escort hold.*

I *The importance of the touch'n'cuff method to control potentially violent subjects.*

I *When to use the team takedown tactic.*

I *Foot pursuits.*

I *Prisoner care.*

Chapter eight

Arrest Skills

ARREST TECHNIQUES

The arrest is a proven flashpoint. It is the moment when the individual knows that the game is up and he or she has one of three choices:

I FIGHT – Assault the officer.

I FLIGHT – Escape from the officer.

I FOLLOW – Comply with instructions.

Always be prepared for the worst and assume that the person may become violent. If the person is already violent, or tries to flee, officers have the following options:

I If the person's identity is known and the offence is not serious the situation may dictate that the officers allow the individual to leave the scene and arrange to arrest him or her later.

I Use communication skills to pacify the individual.

I Use some form of restraint, either a defensive tactic, rigid handcuff or baton technique.

I Use a team takedown tactic if there are two or more officers.

I If appropriate call for PSU trained and equipped officers to perform the 'violent person' tactic.

THE ARREST – PRACTICAL APPLICATION

Police officers may have already lost the reactionary gap by searching at close quarters, ie, within punching/kicking distance. They should be at the side of, or at the rear of, the person – not in front.

THE 'PASSIVE' SUBJECT

Remembering that no situation can be classified as 'low risk' from an officer safety perspective, anticipate that any person can present a risk. The ability to use an edged weapon to kill is not dependent upon such factors as gender, age or strength. At the point of a knife virtually anyone can exert tonnes of pressure per square centimetre – **anyone has the ability to stab with an edged weapon!** In the writer's research people who have assaulted police officers range in age from 12 years to 66 years.

Assess the subject, environment and available resources before considering the options available:

I Should the officers restrain the person before announcing that he or she is under arrest?

I Can the use of handcuffs be justified?

I If the officers decided not to handcuff the subject could they account for their reasons not to handcuff?

Police training and experience of arrests may lull officers into thinking that the correct procedure is to tell the person he is under arrest before taking hold of him. This is not always a safe sequence. An apparently passive individual when arrested may make use of the delay in restraining him to resist arrest.

In some cases it will be safer to restrain the person first and only then announce he has been arrested. It is safer for the officer, and therefore safer for the individual. If loose prisoner handling results in a messy restraint, injuries can be inflicted on police officers. Two ways of restraining a passive subject are:

I The escort hold, or

I the application of handcuffs.

THE ESCORT HOLD

Approach the person from the rear at the 4 o'clock or 8 o'clock position and take hold of his wrist and upper arm. Slightly bend the subject's elbow and wrist to make any restraint techniques easier to apply if they become necessary. A passive individual will allow an officer to maintain this hold and comply with instructions.

If the person resists this is a serious escalation of the situation requiring an immediate response. Officers may decide to push the person away at the same time as stepping back to gain a reactionary gap. Officers are then left in a situation where they have an aggressive individual who has been arrested, but not controlled. Experience indicates that to move in and restrain such a man or woman is likely to have a negative outcome, ie, either the officer and/or the individual will be injured.

Resistance from individuals can come in several forms:

I They may lock their elbow and stiffen their arm.

I They may bend their arm in towards their body.

I They may use threatening language towards the officer detailing the consequences of not letting go.

The escort hold.

Prisoner resists the escort hold.

Officer performs a knee strike to the prisoner's thigh.

The officer straightens the prisoner's arm, turning it palm uppermost.

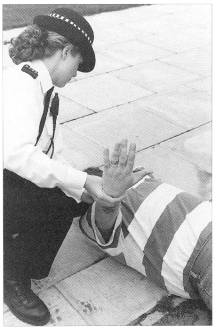

The officer pushes the prisoner forward onto the ground.

The officer keeps the arm locked out straight and moves it into a vertical position for handcuffing.

Some people may be 'hold wise'. They may have been arrested previously and know what restraints are applied. The resisting prisoner is a serious threat to the safety of the officer and immediate action is required to control and restrain the individual quickly. By locking his arm the officer is unlikely to be able to apply any intricate technique on him. One method to control the prisoner is a knee strike. (Other methods of control are the transport or entangled armlocks and the forearm strike as taught in the defensive tactics package.)

Keeping hold of the arm the officer strikes the prisoner's nearest upper thigh with her knee. This causes the person to be distracted, stunned, experience discomfort, possibly lose balance and suffer temporary motor dysfunction (a 'dead leg'). The objective of the knee strike is to regain control, it is not a punishment.

The officer now has to restrain the prisoner, which is most effectively done once he has been placed on the floor in the prone position (face down). To effect this the officer pulls the controlled hand across her hip and turns the hand palm uppermost, locking the arm by placing her hand above the individual's elbow.

Keeping a downward pressure on the arm she gives clear and loud verbal commands, 'Down!, down!, down!,' or 'Get down now!' The officer maintains her balance and keeps the arm locked out straight, all the way to the ground.

To complete the technique the officer must still handcuff the prisoner and prevent him from getting up. She rotates and places her knee on top of the prisoner's shoulder blade keeping the arm locked out and the controlled hand in a wrist lock.

If the officer drops her weight onto the prisoner's shoulder this could cause injury to the shoulder joint. Also keeping pressure on the chest could lead to asphyxia. Once the individual has been handcuffed at the rear he must be searched thoroughly and assisted to stand. Care should be exercised when getting the prisoner to his feet. Officers can roll the prisoners over and push them forwards towards their bent knee (see the High Risk Prone Search in the Search Skill chapter).

THE TOUCH'N'CUFF METHOD

Before handcuffs can be applied there must be some objective grounds to justify their use. Instructions for the use of handcuffs state:

'The decision to use them will generally be at the discretion of the individual officer and although it is not possible to give instructions to cover every eventuality there must be some objective basis for the decision. The safety of the public and police officers, and the security of the prisoner are important considerations.

'Officers may use handcuffs when dealing with violent, or potentially violent persons who have been arrested or detained on reasonable grounds, or with a prisoner who is likely to escape.

'Use should be as discreet as possible and in every case where they are used a notebook... entry must be made and brought to the attention of the custody officer.

'In every instance where handcuffs are put on a prisoner they must be double-locked unless it is clearly impracticable to do so, for example if the prisoner is struggling or violent. In every case where handcuffs are not double-locked frequent checks should be made to ensure that the circulation is not restricted and no unnecessary injury is caused.

'Only in exceptional circumstances should handcuffs be used on elderly persons, juveniles, mental health cases or those committed to prison for non-payment of fines imposed on summary conviction.'

Can you state the reasons why you applied handcuffs? Although there must be some genuine grounds for handcuffs the person need not be a raging bull before police officers consider handcuffs necessary. In fact, it prevents injury for all concerned if handcuffs are put on before a person has a violent outburst.

Rather than taking hold of prisoners in the escort hold and using techniques to restrain them sufficiently to handcuff them, a touch'n'cuff method may be preferable. Touch'n'cuff is simply the way simultaneously to apply one handcuff the instant an officer touches a prisoner for the first time. Use this method with approved rigid handcuff techniques. The objective of touch'n'cuff is to take the initiative swiftly before the prisoner has time to react. The use of handcuffs must be justified and officers should be equipped with rigid handcuffs to achieve control.

As an example officers can use touch'n'cuff with the Quik-Kuf 'Strong-side push, bottom cuff' technique as follows when arresting individuals who are potentially violent:

I The officer moves into close quarters on the left side of the individual (this example uses a right-handed officer.)

I She maintains the correct stance and covertly draws her rigid handcuffs (the low profile draw) so as not to signal her intention to apply handcuffs.

I The officer takes hold of the person's left hand and **simultaneously** snaps the bottom cuff onto the wrist from the little finger side.

I She takes control of the prisoner by tightening the bottom cuff with her weak hand; pushing the top cuff with her strong hand; and using verbal commands. At this point she informs the prisoner that he is under arrest.

I The officer takes hold of the handcuffs in her weak hand and rotates them in a large anti-clockwise circle.

I The officer then secures the prisoner's other hand in the handcuffs.

I The officer checks the handcuffs for tightness.

I Finally, the officer double-locks the handcuffs to stop them tightening up in transit. She uses the tip of a ball-point pen to depress the double-locking pins instead of rummaging for one of her handcuff keys. **It is essential that she carries at least one handcuff key with her**.

The actual handcuffing technique is the same as taught in the Quik-Kuf training programme. Touch'n'cuff simply means snapping the first cuff on before the prisoner has had time to react.

It is important not to convey the intention to handcuff by overtly drawing handcuffs or telling the prisoner that he is under arrest until one cuff has been applied properly. The success of the tactic depends on speed. If it does not work first time use another technique such as an escort hold, team takedown or baton technique.

The officer applies the bottom cuff the instant she touches the prisoner.

The officer achieves control of the prisoner.

By rotating the handcuffs anti-clockwise the subject is turned away from the officer.

The prisoner's hands are secured in a back to back position.

The officer uses the tip of her forefinger to check tightness between the handcuff and the prisoner's wrist.

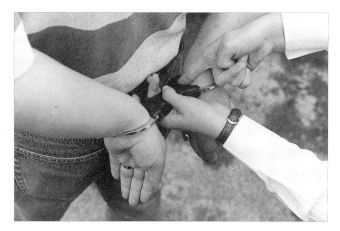

The officer double-locks the handcuffs with the tip of a ball-point pen.

THE TEAM TAKEDOWN

Ideally the team takedown, or swarm technique, directly involves four officers. Any additional officer in attendance will cover the team from any bystanders who attempt to intervene. The team of officers overpower the person physically. An alternative option would be baton techniques if these are justified in the circumstances. In practice when two or more officers have to arrest a disorderly individual they still tend to use some form of overpowering tactic rather than baton techniques. The takedown technique should be used where attempts to communicate have failed to ensure compliance and the individual is not believed to be armed.

Ideally the environment should allow the officers to encircle the person. It is not suitable for use in a confined space, such as a cell. The officer who has been communicating will usually lead the technique regardless of rank. The technique can be used with three or even two officers, but the chances of an officer being injured may increase if fewer than four officers are used. The physical presence of four officers may be enough to achieve compliance.

The team surrounds the subject.

The subject is rushed; tackled from behind and his arms restrained.

The subject's limbs are restrained.

Officer ready to protect her colleagues from interference from any bystanders.

The technique must have been practised or at least talked through beforehand to ensure that the team know what they are going to do. **The aim is for the person to be restrained on the ground in a prone position face down, ensuring maximum safety for all concerned**.

❚ All the team keep a reactionary gap from the person.

❚ The leader keeps a dialogue going clearly requesting compliance loudly enough for the individual and any bystanders to hear.

❚ The other three team members encircle the person without communicating with him. Ideally one officer should be directly behind the subject at the *6 o'clock* position and one on either side.

❚ When the team is in position the leader gives a pre-arranged signal to rush the individual.

❚ The officer at the *6 o'clock* position will rugby tackle the person's legs at knee level whilst the officers at each side control the arm nearest them. The leg officer will try and lock the knees together by gripping his own elbows. (It is essential to control the legs and officers must expect to get their uniforms dirty.)

❚ The individual is forced to the ground. If the individual is face up and still resisting the leader moves in, holds the head and gives a verbal command, 'Stop!'. The team maintain their holds and follow the commands of the leader to roll the subject over, etc.

❚ If possible the leader should continue to hold the individual's head to prevent accidental or self-inflicted facial injury being caused.

❚ The arms should be restrained by application of wristlocks if necessary and the hands cuffed behind the back; remembering to check the tightness of the handcuffs and double locking them.

❚ If the person is still struggling remove his footwear (it is less effective to kick out in bare feet than it is with footwear on).

❚ Other officers not needed to restrain the prisoner should protect the team from bystanders intervening. These officers could explain the necessity of the team takedown tactic to placate any onlookers.

Safety Factors

❚ When holding the head to prevent injury, do not let the prisoner have the opportunity of biting police officers and do not hold the subject around the throat or neck.

❚ Placing weight on the prisoner's back will cause him breathing difficulties. Should the prisoner still be struggling restrain his limbs, do not sit on his back.

❚ Ensure that the safety of the prisoner is considered. Monitor the airway, breathing and circulation. If the prisoner is experiencing breathing difficulties act straight away. If he is lying face down sit him up or turn him on his side immediately.

I Request an ambulance if the prisoner requires urgent medical attention. Ask him if he has any medical condition or has taken drugs.

I When transporting a prisoner keep him seated and under observation. On arrival at the police station tell the custody officer of any medical condition or drugs by which that the prisoner may be affected.

I Restraints are applied to ensure compliance. If the technique hurts all the time then the individual has nothing to lose by continuing to struggle. He may also get an adrenaline rush which will give him extra short term energy. Relax restraint holds when the individual complies with verbal commands.

Readers might think, 'Why not use a baton technique?' In practice police officers still opt for an overpowering technique to get a person onto the ground instead of a baton technique. Research from the San Diego Police Department has shown that team takedowns were nearly twice as effective at restraining emotionally disturbed people than baton techniques.

Flexibility is essential for this tactic to work, as real life incidents do not allow for rigid adherence to a blueprint. The team takedown tactic is very fluid and officers may find themselves out of position; if this occurs they will have to restrain the prisoner quickly as best they can.

If just two officers use this tactic one will still take the legs whilst the other takes an arm. If the leg officer is tackling from the side he or she must make sure that they place their head **behind** the individual's knees – not in front of them. Police officers may be reluctant to get their highly polished footwear scuffed or their neatly pressed uniform soiled; in the team takedown they must expect to end up on the ground.

Edged Weapon

If a individual has, or is believed to have, an edged weapon do not use the team takedown tactic. An edged weapon, unless thrown, is only dangerous if the individual can get within striking range.

Employ the CUT system from the Weapon Threat chapter. Communicate with the individual if it can be done safely. Get protective equipment, knife resistant body armour and gloves and public order helmets, at least.

An appropriate tactic to deal with an individual armed with an edged weapon may be the 'violent person' tactic used by public order personnel. This is done with protective equipment and trained officers. It is labour intensive and will need a minimum of **nine** officers organised in three teams of three.

In time a less than lethal weapon may be available to overpower safely someone armed with an edged weapon.

FOOT PURSUIT

Keeping a safe reactionary gap does allow individuals a head start if they decide to flee. Before engaging in a foot pursuit assess the situation.

The subject may have no good reason for running off and simply be mischievous.

On a more sinister level he may be trying to lure police officers into some sort of ambush or separate an officer from his or her vehicle to damage it.

Objective
1. Survive.
2. Detection of crime and the arrest of offenders –
   the individual may be wanted or have incriminating articles on him.

Subject – Consider:
1. The physical ability, speed and strength of the person relative to you.
2. The seriousness of the offence he has committed.

Environment – Consider:
1. Hazards such as passing traffic, building sites, railway lines and water features, eg, canals and rivers.
2. High tension area (poor police community relations where assistance for the police is unlikely).

Self – Consider:
1. Your physical fitness and fatigue level to catch and restrain.
2. Your local knowledge of the area.
3. Whether you have a backup officer or are on solo patrol.

Options
1. Pursue on foot.
2. Report to control, cordon and attempt to intercept.

Fitness

People who flee could well be significantly younger than the police officers attempting to pursue them. They may well be wearing training shoes, be uncluttered with equipment and have a surge of adrenaline pumping around their bodies. Officers have to have the speed to catch the individuals and, importantly, the strength to restrain them when arrested. Do not take unnecessary risks whilst in pursuit, like running across a building site at night. When running the baton should be carried in the strong-hand, this will save it bouncing about and it will be ready should it be needed.

A foot pursuit can be hazardous and is a severe test of an officer's fitness.

'He must be around here somewhere.'

Communication

The control room require the following information:

I Your location.

I The subject's direction of travel.

I A brief description of the subject.

I The offence committed.

I Any weapon which the subject may be carrying.

It is hard to transmit coherently whilst running. If there are two officers in the pursuit the slower officer should use the radio whilst keeping the faster one in sight. The faster officer should concentrate on catching up with the individual whilst the slower officer should keep the control room informed of progress.

Technique

The most dangerous aspect of a pursuit is when visual contact with those pursued is lost. They may be desperate criminals prepared to assault police officers rather than being captured.

Stay together as a team when a person is lost sight of. The chances of finding the individual are obviously improved if officers split up, but it is far easier for the person to attack officers singly rather than together.

Assume that the individual may well have picked up some object to use as a weapon and is waiting around the next corner or behind the next wall.

Take care when rounding corners or crossing obstacles, such as walls. Take a wide route around a corner to increase your vision. Take precautions before crossing any wall. Listen for sounds of movement. Do not cross in the same place as the subject. Consider hazards on the other side of the wall.

If the pursuit has entered a tense (hard to police) area it may be safer to discontinue the pursuit and organise a cordon. Consider the deployment of police dog handlers and air support.

The Arrest

The safest method of stopping the individual is to push him in the back causing him to fall over or take them to the ground with an armlock. A rugby tackle will leave both the officer and the suspect on the ground and is not recommended as it is not possible to predict who will end up on top.

Once the individual is on the ground use verbal commands so that he or she lies face down, palms up and legs crossed. Handcuff the person behind the back and conduct a thorough search.

A search of the route should be made to recover any discarded articles.

PRISONER CARE

The primary mission of the police service is public safety. This means officer safety as well as the safety of the public and prisoners.

Because a particular self-defence hold, baton technique, or handcuff technique is recognised in an approved training programme does not absolve officers from having to justify its use. If officers apply such an approved technique to a person and the circumstances do not warrant such a level of force the officers may face criminal, civil or disciplinary hearings and be asked to justify their actions.

By the same token, if police officers use a technique which they have improvised to restrain a subject it is not automatically unlawful providing they can justify its use, bearing in mind section 3 of the Criminal Law Act 1967.

In a democracy officers are accountable to the public and have to bear in mind public opinion. There are probably some extremely efficient techniques known to martial arts experts at incapacitating another person but they would be totally unacceptable to the police service and the public as permanent disability is likely. It would be unrealistic for the police service to prohibit every possible technique other than those taught in their training programmes. The first person responsible for justifying the use of any technique, whether approved or improvised, will be the officer applying the technique.

In practice officers use techniques which work for them. They are either approved techniques, improvised techniques or a mixture of both. Whilst improvised techniques are not unlawful per se, certain points should be borne in mind.

Firstly, it should be easier to justify the application of an approved technique. The organisation may possibly be able to provide an expert witness with knowledge of training to explain the technique. With an improvised technique officers may be on their own.

Secondly, police officers should be aware of the dangers when applying an improvised technique. If the officers have applied such a technique to someone who is struggling violently how do they know that the person has stopped struggling in order to attack them and is now struggling to survive. One basic physiological need is a supply of oxygen and individuals can be deprived of oxygen in two ways:

I By the mouth or windpipe being obstructed.

I The inability to inflate and deflate the lungs due to the persons posture.

Therefore asphyxia can be caused by a choke hold around someone's throat, weight being placed on his back or by him lying on his front. When someone is placed face down the ability to breathe is hampered because the stomach is forced upwards towards the chest. This is most acute in overweight people. Also if the individual is drunk, drugged, exhausted or has a heart or lung condition he is at risk from positional (or postural) asphyxia. Lack of oxygen can lead to a cardiac arrest followed by death. Review the safety factors regarding the team takedown tactic to prevent positional asphyxia.

Tragedies can occur where there are several officers attempting to restrain an extremely violent individual. There is often a vicious cycle where a violent individual is restrained face down and weight placed on his or her back. The individual has difficulty breathing and struggles for air; the officers apply more force to overcome the individual. It is important therefore that officers practice working together to restrain a single individual safely.

Neck-holds can prove fatal. Many individuals have died due to neck-holds being applied. There are two schools of thought on the subject. There are those who believe that neck-holds can be applied safely, given appropriate training. Others believe that the risks are too great to recommend their use. Neck-holds are not in the ACPO training package; they are not approved techniques. The writer does not recommend the use of neck-holds.

Unfortunately neck-holds will continue to be used by officers on the streets, as they may have no other alternative. Officers must be under no illusion that they need to justify their actions in applying neck-holds bearing in mind the behaviour of the individual and the impact factors.

SUMMARY

The point of arrest is a common flashpoint often leading to assaults on police officers.

For officers to deal professionally with people who resist violently they must develop skills in arrest techniques.

Each time officers have to control someone physically they should review the event and look for ways of improving their performance.

Chapter nine

ESCORT SKILLS

KEYPOINTS

Use this chapter to find out:

▌ *How to escort prisoners safely on foot and in vehicles.*

▌ *How to use the cell relocation tactic.*

▌ *How to un-handcuff safely.*

Chapter nine

Escort Skills

INTRODUCTION

Approximately a quarter of assaults on police officers occur after the prisoners have been arrested and are being escorted to the police station. Safe prisoner handling techniques reduce the risk of assault.

Many good arrests are spoilt by poor prisoner handling. The incident may have been dealt with well until the arrest. Officers then have a tendency to 'switch off' and relax, thinking that the incident is all over. It is during the escort phase to the police station that the prisoner becomes violent or tries to escape. As the officers get closer to the police station they may feel more relaxed; the prisoners, however, could well be getting increasingly anxious. The watchful prisoners see opportunities to hit back at the officers or break free. Maybe the officers turned their backs on the prisoners or the prisoners were not restrained.

It is crucial that officers do not ruin all their good work in resolving incidents by poor escort skills.

ESCORTING A PRISONER ON FOOT

Officers should always be aware of relative positioning when escorting a prisoner on foot. This means keeping out of the prisoner's fighting arc (*10 o'clock* to *2 o'clock*). Take up the escort position on both sides of the prisoner and gain control by holding the prisoner's upper arm. Use verbal commands to direct the prisoner, making sure that the prisoner's fighting arc does not present a danger to anyone else.

Public order trained officers are proficient in other tactics for escorting aggressive individuals on foot. These are not covered by this book as they require appropriate training and practice.

VEHICLE TRANSPORTATION

Ideally, prior to being escorted in a vehicle, the prisoner must be properly handcuffed and searched. The most dangerous combination is the prisoner who has not been searched or handcuffed.

Passive prisoners may be transported in the rear of a patrol car. The rear doors must have their child locks on. Sit the prisoner behind the front passenger seat, not behind the driver. An escorting officer should sit next to the prisoner and ensure that the prisoner is restrained by the rear seat belt. Do not lean in front of the prisoner to put the seat belt on.

Escorting a subject on foot.   *The escort officer should be prepared for any resistance from the prisoner.*

In the event of one male officer escorting one female prisoner in a vehicle it would be wise to request the control room to log on the computer incident the exact mileage on the patrol car's odometer at the start of the journey. Give updates to the control room if the journey is lengthy. On arrival at the police station request the control room to log the exact finish mileage and time. This may assist the officer if the female makes a spurious complaint that the officer made a detour from the route to commit an act of impropriety.

Clearly it is far better for a female officer to escort a female prisoner. Failing that, two male officers may escort a female prisoner, but this is still not an ideal solution. The most unsatisfactory option is one male officer escorting a female prisoner.

Violent, or potentially violent, prisoners should only be transported in the rear of a car if a personnel carrier is not available. Where prisoners have been struggling violently, consider removing their footwear. For safety reasons officers must have the prisoner's foot pinned to the ground whilst doing this. Someone without shoes is less inclined to kick the windows or panels of a vehicle.

It is always safer to transport prisoners (whether violent or passive) in a caged personnel carrier than in a car.

In extreme cases a prisoner may have to be physically restrained in transit. Care should be taken not to cause asphyxia. Only restrain him in a seated position, not a prone position. Review the prisoner care section of the previous chapter.

Loose articles should not be within reach of prisoners being transported in police vehicles. Search vehicles which have been used to transport prisoners, especially if there has been any opportunity for them to hide property by not being monitored constantly.

Some general guidance regarding transportation of prisoners:

▌ Never handcuff a prisoner to:
   A fixed object or,
   a police officer.

▌ Avoid handcuffing two prisoners together. If this is not practical then handcuff them right hand to right hand to make running more awkward.

▌ If possible do not transport in the same vehicle:
   The defendant and the aggrieved person.
   A male and a female.
   An adult and a juvenile.
   People who have displayed violent behaviour towards each other.

▌ Do not:
   Carry more than two prisoners in the rear of a patrol car with an escort behind the driver.
   Carry the prisoner in the front passenger seat.
   Carry a prisoner in the back of an unscreened vehicle if on solo patrol.

▌ When taking charge of a prisoner from another officer always search the prisoner.

▌ When officers reach the custody area search the subject thoroughly **before** removing the handcuffs.

▌ Adopt the safe un-handcuffing procedure – explained later in this chapter.

CELL RELOCATION

The cell relocation technique is a team tactic which is widely used in the Prison Service requiring three officers. It is only to be used where the prisoner is so violent that to use any other technique would expose the officers to an unacceptably high risk of being injured. It is primarily intended to be used in custody areas to move a prisoner from one area to another.

The technique starts with the prisoner face down in the prone position with his hands properly handcuffed behind him. The prisoner will be in that position following a take down technique, such as the 'violent person' technique used by trained public order personnel. Police officers may also be able to justify using this on the streets to transport a violent prisoner from the point of arrest through to the custody area.

Step One

With the prisoner prone, face down and handcuffed to the rear, one officer takes control of the prisoner's head. That officer is the leader and in charge of the technique and will be the only one to give commands. The leader must direct any additional officers in the vicinity to protect the team from interference from bystanders if in a public place. It is important that the leader ensures that the prisoner does not injure himself by head butting the ground. This officer must also be mindful that he does not restrict the blood supply or airway of the prisoner by applying pressure to the neck area. The officer must keep his hands clear of the prisoner's mouth in case he tries to bite.

One officer will kneel at either side of the prisoner facing each other. Their arms closest to the prisoner's head will go under the shoulder joint to support it. Their arms nearest to the prisoner's feet will slide under the handcuffed arms and they will place their palms on the top of the prisoner's shoulder blades.

Prisoner restrained.

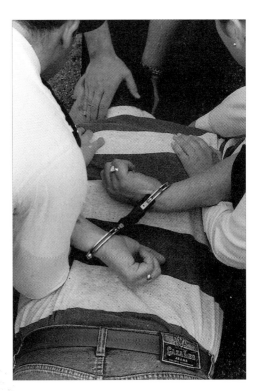

Step Two

When the leader is satisfied that the shoulders are supported by the other officers he instructs the prisoner to get onto his knees, 'Listen. We're going to help you up. Get your knees up towards your stomach'. As the prisoner starts to get up onto his knees the officers at either side support and lift the prisoner's shoulders from **underneath**.

When the prisoner has got onto his knees the leader instructs the prisoner to stand up. The leader now goes on ahead to clear the access for the team.

Step Three

When the team enters a cell they ensure it is done so that the prisoner's head is closest to the door. The leader takes hold of the prisoner's head and again instructs the prisoner to get down onto his knees. The officers either side support the prisoner's shoulders from underneath and the leader gives the prisoner a verbal command, 'Turn your head to the side. Now go down onto your front'.

The prisoner will now have to be searched thoroughly. Whilst the two officers at each side keep control of the prisoner the leader searches the back of the prisoner from head to toe, taking particular care not to be kicked by the prisoner. Once this is done the leader and the left side officer stand around the back of the right side officer to minimise the risk of being kicked or bitten. The right side officer then pulls the prisoner over onto his side.

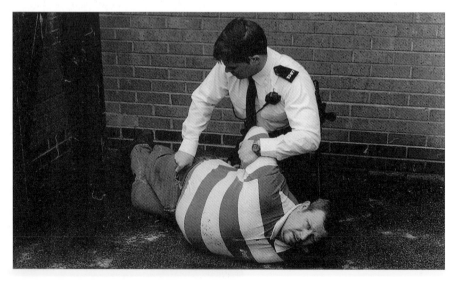

When searching the prisoner care must be taken to minimise the risk of injury to his wrists when using rigid handcuffs.

There are dangers to the health of the prisoner who is in the prone position. Officers must understand these dangers by reviewing the prisoner care section in the previous chapter.

Keeping the prisoner on his side the officer searches the prisoner thoroughly from the stomach to the head with the right hand. The left hand stabilises the prisoner in this position. Once the upper body has been searched the officer takes hold of the elbow with the right hand and searches from the prisoner's stomach to his feet with the left hand. A verbal command, 'Bend your leg', will ensure that the officer does not have to stretch down to search right to the foot.

When this officer is satisfied with the search the prisoner should be returned to the face down position so the left side officer can take over and conduct a search of the other side of the prisoner's body using the same procedure

Once the prisoner has been searched and is back in the face down, prone position the two officers either side apply wrist locks. Any loose items should be removed from the cell. The leader should check that the cell door lock is in the ready position so that it can be closed swiftly.

The leader removes each handcuff ensuring that the side officers maintain the wrist locks. The leader keeps the verbal communication going, eg,

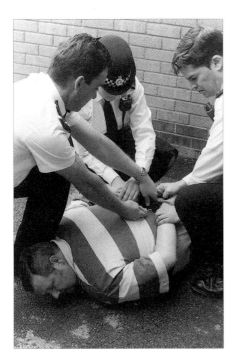

Removing the handcuffs while applying wristlocks to the prisoner.

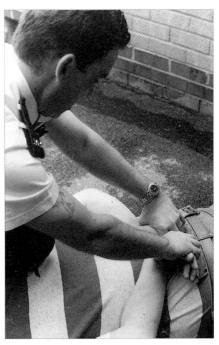

The leader takes control of both wristlocks.

'Just relax. It'll be over soon'. The leader reholsters the handcuffs and takes over the pressure on both wrist locks. Without any word of command the leader signals by a nod of the head for each side officer to leave the cell.

The leader is left applying both wristlocks. When the leader is ready he springs backwards and vacate the cell. If done correctly the prisoner will be too fatigued to offer any immediate resistance thus giving the leader time to escape from the cell.

The custody officer must be made aware of the technique applied and regular checks on the prisoner must be made. This technique is invaluable when dealing with violent prisoners. It works. Ideally all police officers should be proficient in this technique. Whoever is proficient should take charge of the team, irrespective of rank.

There are variations to this technique. The training which police officers receive may therefore be slightly different to that described above.

UNCUFFING A PRISONER

Even an apparently passive prisoner may take advantage of being uncuffed to attack police officers. If the prisoner has been violent it may be safer to have the prisoner lying down in the cell before taking the handcuffs off. In other cases, to un-handcuff safely officers must control the prisoner so he cannot assault them.

The prisoner must have been searched before the handcuffs are removed. Stand the prisoner about one and a half feet away from a smooth wall. The officer secures the prisoner's nearest foot by placing his foot on it. He then gets the prisoner to face away from him and leans him forward onto the wall. The officer will place his hand against the prisoner's cheek to prevent facial injury. When the prisoner's chest is against the wall the officer can start the un-handcuffing process.

The officer gently leans his shoulder against the middle of the prisoner's back and tells the prisoner that as soon as one hand is free he must reach out and place it (palm outwards) against the wall. The officer keeps his own head down to prevent the prisoner headbutting him. As with all un-handcuffing procedures the officer removes the handcuff furthest away from him first.

Finally the officer removes the other handcuff and steps back.

The officer maintains control of the handcuffs throughout the procedure. If the prisoner is about to attack the officer when the first handcuff is removed he can be easily controlled. Do not push the prisoner to the floor if he still has both hands handcuffed as a back injury may result.

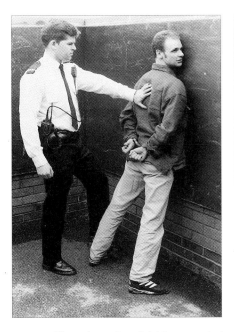

The prisoner's weight is supported
by the wall.

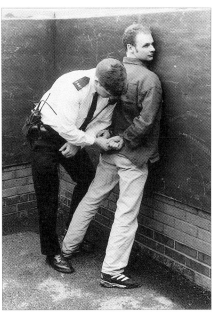

The officer stabilises the prisoner by
leaning against his back while removing
the furthest handcuff first.

Once the prisoner has placed his free arm
against the wall (palm out) the officer
removes the other handcuff.

The officer keeps behind the subject
at all times.

CUSTODY AREA

The custody area is a volatile arena. The writer suspects that many minor assaults on police officers and civilian detention officers go unreported as the offenders are already on remand or are convicted and it is not considered worthwhile to pursue the offence. A prisoner is always a risk until the cell door closes.

When escorting prisoners in the custody area always stay in the escort position, ie, the *4 o'clock* or *8 o'clock* position.

Officers should be aware of their stance with regard to the prisoner.

❙ Do not let the prisoner get on your baton side.

❙ Do not turn your back on a prisoner.

❙ Be aware of the location of panic buttons in the custody area.

SUMMARY

Just because the prisoner has been arrested the incident is not 'over' until he or she is secured in a police cell.

Remain alert to the possibility that the prisoner may be ready to assault police officers in order to escape.

Practice safe escort and un-handcuffing techniques and use them.

Chapter ten

WEAPON THREAT

KEYPOINTS

Use this chapter to find out:

I *What are the characteristics of firearms.*

I *What are the dangers associated with edged weapons.*

I *What immediate action should be taken when facing an armed person.*

Chapter ten

Weapon Threat

FIREARM THREAT

The most common firearms which police officers are likely to encounter on Britain's streets are shotguns and handguns. This section concentrates on these types of weapon and the characteristics of the ammunition they fire.

Becoming increasingly more common are sub-machine guns, especially when encountered in the possession of drug gangs. Less common, but which could become more popular, are weapons from Eastern Europe, for example the Kalashnikov assault rifle.

From an officer safety point of view, the most dangerous type of firearm is the rifle. A rifle is more accurate than other weapons and the ammunition is more powerful. The amount of cover required in order to be protected from a rifle is substantial, eg, a thick brick built wall would be a minimum. If there is any doubt about what type of firearm is involved in an incident the safest course of action is to assume that the firearm is a rifle and act accordingly.

SHOTGUNS

The most common type of double-barrelled shotgun is called the 'side by side'. The other type has one barrel on top of the other and is called the 'under and over'.

Both these shotguns have to be opened for the user to extract the spent cartridges and reload the barrels with fresh cartridges.

Criminals illegally shorten the barrels and stocks of these shotguns to create 'sawn offs'. Although accuracy may diminish the 'sawn off' can be more easily concealed and is a devastating weapon.

The 'pump action' shotgun is single barrelled and holds several fresh cartridges in a tubular magazine which runs parallel with the barrel. The weapon is reloaded by sliding the action backwards and forwards which ejects the used cartridge and chambers a fresh one from the magazine. Legislation has reduced the magazine capacity of these shotguns, but they can be modified illegally to hold six or more cartridges. They can sustain a higher rate of fire than more conventional shotguns as they are quicker to reload.

Shotguns can be loaded with a variety of cartridges. These range from 'birdshot' which contain approximately 250 tiny lead pellets, through to a cartridge which contains a single lead shot. Birdshot inflicts massive

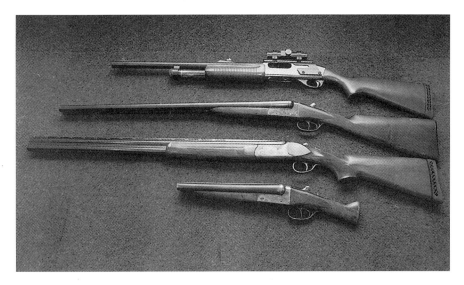

Types of shotgun. Pump action. Side by side. Under and over. Sawn off.

wounds to humans at close range and can be fatal. They can easily penetrate the bodywork of a car.

An SSG shotgun cartridge (also called 'Double O Buckshot') contains 9
lead shot each 0.3" in diameter. The shot spreads out one inch each yard
travelled. At 50 yards therefore the shot will have spread to cover an area
of at least four feet in diameter. Needless to say this ammunition is lethal.
Cartridges with several shot can still cause injury at a range of half a mile.

The single lead shot is called the rifled slug. The lead slug's outer casing
is rifled so that when it is fired through the smooth bore barrel of a shotgun the rifling on the slug spins it to give it stability in flight and therefore greater accuracy. It is such a devastating cartridge that the police use
it solely for destroying large wild animals. It is lethal to human targets.
Although not sold commercially in Britain it can be obtained overseas. In
addition to commercially manufactured cartridges criminals have chosen
to load their own cartridges with a variety of lethal objects.

Buckshot and rifled slug cartridges.

HANDGUNS

Handguns come in two varieties, revolvers and self-loading pistols (although technically they function as semi-automatics they are more commonly referred to as 'automatics').

Revolvers normally hold five or six rounds and are very reliable. Should a round fail to discharge the firer simply has to pull the trigger again to fire the next round. Due to the strength of the weapons they are capable of discharging powerful rounds, often called magnums, for example the .357" Magnum. Revolvers are slow to reload unless the firer has a speed-loader to replenish all the rounds at once.

Automatics can hold as many as 15 or more rounds. They require greater proficiency by the firer and a misfire takes longer to rectify than with a revolver. Due to the firing action an automatic cannot fire the powerful magnum rounds, but makes up for this by a higher rate of fire. It can be reloaded more quickly than a revolver as the firer simply replaces the empty magazine with a full one. Typical ammunition for an automatic is the military 9mm round.

A handgun round can still cause injury at a range of at least a mile.

Above: Revolver and automatic pistols.

Left: 9mm cartridges commonly used in automatics and .38" cartridges used in revolvers.

OTHER FIREARMS

Sub-machine guns (sometimes called machine carbines) have also appeared on Britain's streets, often associated with the drug culture. These have similar firing actions to automatics. They can usually fire fully automatic, ie, once the trigger has been pulled the weapon will continue to fire unless the pressure is released from the trigger or the magazine is emptied. Some are restricted to single shot, ie, each time the trigger is pulled the weapon fires only once. The advantage of sub-machine guns is that they are more stable and accurate than an automatic handgun, due to the increased weight and barrel length. The magazine capacity is usually greater than that of an automatic handgun, normally 30 or more rounds. This type of weapon can sustain a very high rate of fire.

Military rifles are capable of firing powerful high velocity ammunition, such as 7.62mm or 5.56mm, which are capable of penetrating standard ballistic body armour. Additional composite plates of metal and ceramic material are required to defeat this type of ammunition. The weapons usually have a high rate of fire, either semi or fully automatic. Due to the long barrel length the rifle is an accurate weapon. In the hands of a well trained user a human target can be engaged at a range of at least 600

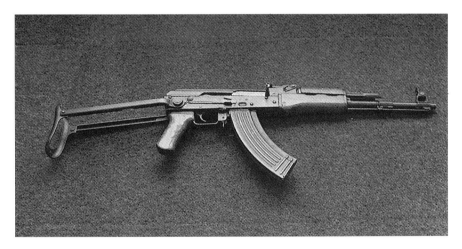

Above: The Kalashnikov AK-47 is a rugged assault rifle capable of fully automatic fire.

Right: These high velocity cartridges are used in military and hunting rifles, 5.56mm and 7.62mm.

metres. The bullet will travel much further (three miles plus) and will still cause injury.

Hunting or sporting rifles can fire military type ammunition. These are very accurate weapons in the hands of an experienced user. The practical range of these weapons is increased when a telescopic sight is fitted. As these rifles are bolt action they have a much lower rate of fire than military rifles.

FIREARM FINDS

When officers find firearms their priority must be public safety. If the weapon can be left in situ, then leave a police officer with it until firearms trained officers arrive to make the weapon safe.

If a firearm must be moved follow these two basic rules:

∎ Do not touch the trigger mechanism.

∎ Keep the muzzle of the weapon pointing in a safe direction at all times.

If the firearm is required for evidential purposes take precautions not to destroy fingerprints or gunpowder residue evidence by unnecessary handling of the weapon. Get expert advice.

Leave cartridges in situ unless it is essential to move them. Do not touch the casings as they often have incriminating fingerprints on them.

IMMEDIATE ACTIONS

Police officers are most at risk when they spontaneously encounter an armed subject at close range. There are two factors in an officer's favour:

∎ It is difficult to hit a fast moving target, especially one that is running laterally (rather than directly away from the firer).

∎ Only one in ten casualties in battle are killed instantaneously by a gunshot wound. Even if someone has been shot they can still keep going if they have a will to survive.

If the individual is intent on shooting (it is safest to assume he or she is) then **flight** or **fight** are an officer's only realistic options.

∎ FLIGHT – Dash for cover. If the firer has taken aim an officer should duck low or drop to one knee to avoid the first shot. Then run fast laterally and dive into bullet proof cover a safe distance away. Do not leave good cover unless absolutely necessary.

∎ FIGHT – Use a pre-emptive attack on the individual if there is no other alternative. Throw a clipboard or hat in his or her face to cause a distraction. Grab the firearm and repeatedly strike the individual as hard and fast as possible. This is a critical life or death moment. This advice is based on encountering an armed suspect. The reader must decide what amounts to 'reasonable force' in this type of situation.

The actions for unarmed officers dealing with incidents which may involve firearms are the 'SIX Cs'

I CONFIRM – Confirm that a firearm is involved and locate the subject, ensuring your own safety.

I COVER – Make use of substantial bullet proof cover. A thick brick wall is a minimum requirement. A vehicle is not bullet proof cover.

I CONTACT – Contact your control room and emphasise that the incident may involve a firearm. Request the supervising officer be informed and request assistance.

I CIVILIANS – Be assertive with civilians to prevent them entering or remaining in danger.

I COLLEAGUES – Be assertive with colleagues to direct them away from danger areas, ie, the line of sight from the subject's location.

I CONTAIN – Without unnecessarily endangering yourself keep the subject under observation.

Cover Awareness

It is good practice to be aware of available cover when approaching incidents.

A car door offers practically no protection whatsoever.

Hedges and fences may provide cover from view, but not from fire.

A substantial brick wall affords good cover.

EDGED WEAPONS

Virtually anything can be, and has been, used as an edged weapon, eg, forks, pens and keys. Any item which is capable of being used by someone else to stab or slash can be an edged weapon.

When compared to firearms, edged weapons capable of inflicting serious injury are easily acquired and concealed. In America a third of officers facing a knife assault are injured. It is highly likely therefore that if an officer is attacked by someone with an edged weapon he or she will be wounded. **Edged weapons are lethal**.

Screwdrivers are the second most common murder weapon in the UK, readers should never underestimate their potential danger.

This 'push knife' was actually concealed on a prisoner at the writer's own police station. The knife can be hidden in the palm and used to stab when the hand is clenched into a fist. Victims may only think they are being punched, until it is too late. If individuals have their hands clenched they could be concealing an edged weapon, such as a 'push knife'.

A penetration of only a few millimetres at the throat can be fatal. A knife with a blade of 40 millimetres (less than two inches) can penetrate vital organs including the heart. Severing a major artery, say at the throat, will cause unconsciousness in seconds and death within a minute or so. A small knife can be as much of a threat as a large one.

How confident can officers be that their last prisoner was searched thoroughly enough to find a weapon such as this 'push knife'?

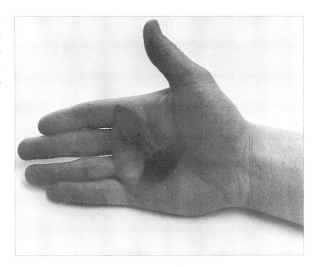

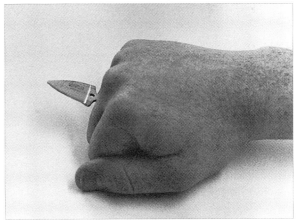

Types of Knives

When one thinks of edged weapons one immediately thinks of knives. There are several knives designed specially for causing injury. All knives can cause slash and stab wounds, but some have been designed specially for stabbing. These knives can cause slashing wounds. In extreme cases they can cause amputation.

All of these knives can cause deep stab wounds. The bayonets, and some daggers, have specially strengthened, or tempered, blades which are not easily damaged.The same company which manufactures the 'push knife', shown above, also sell fibre glass-filled plastic knives to the public by mail order. Although the knives are unsuitable for slashing they can cause stab wounds. The advantage for the criminal is that these knives will not be discovered by metal detectors. Officers should bear this in mind if they are sweeping individuals with hand held metal detectors.

Above left & right: Sheath knives, sometimes called Bowie knives, and machetes.

Left & below: The bayonets are identifiable by the ring which attaches them to firearms. The daggers have a double blade. The flick knives have spring loaded blades.

The use of knives and other edged weapons by criminals is likely to continue:

■ Knives do not jam or run out of ammunition.

■ Criminals do not need to be skilled in their use for them to be lethal.

■ Blades cause large wound tracts and cut flesh, blood vessels and even bone.

■ At close quarters knives are as deadly as firearms.

■ Knives are easy to obtain and hide and are silent in operation.

■ The penalties for carrying edged weapons are far less than for carrying firearms.

There are many advantages for criminals who carry knives and so few disadvantages.

Common Misconceptions about Edged Weapons

■ 'Size is important' – A small knife is easier to conceal than a large one and may cut police officers before they realise what has happened. Small knives can kill just as effectively as big ones.

■ 'You've got to be an expert to use a blade' – Anyone who holds an edged weapon is a serious threat to police officers' lives, whether the user is an expert or not.

■ 'If you get stabbed that's it. You're dead!' – It is rare for someone to die from a single knife wound unless it is to a vital area. Only three per cent of knife assaults prove fatal for police officers. Officers must concentrate on preventing a fatal stab to a vital area, even if they have already been cut.

EQUIPMENT

The Kevlar type ballistic body armour and gloves provide some protection against slashing attacks. Knife resistant body armour tested to the PSDB 42 joule test provides protection against slashing and stabbing attacks. This type of body armour tends to be much less flexible than the ballistic variety. If the body armour is worn overtly, ie, over the uniform, an assailant may well attack the throat or lower abdomen area which is unprotected.

Body armour gives a last line of defence, or buys time to respond, if attacked unexpectedly. Keep out of reach of the attacker and improve the chances of survival.

Use the 'CUT' Immediate Action to avoid injury.

THE 'CUT' IMMEDIATE ACTION

Police officers must use the 'CUT' immediate action to improve their survival when faced with subjects armed with edged weapons:

▌ CREATE DISTANCE – Establish a reactionary gap, a safe distance between the officer and the individual which can be 20 feet or more (the length of two Mini cars). The subject can be dissuaded from closing the gap by verbal commands, baton spins or an incapacitant spray.

▌ USE COVER – Separate the subject from the officer with a physical barrier, door, wall, desk or vehicle.

▌ TRANSMIT – Contact control and request officers with protective equipment. Armed response vehicles and dog handlers could be considered.

(The 'CUT' immediate action has been used with the kind permission of Inspector JC Davison, Metropolitan Police Service.)

Watch the assailant's hands. Stay alert – state red (see Chapter Two – States of Survival Awareness). Expect to get cut, but do not give up.

Trying to tackle a knife-wielding individual single-handed with a baton needs careful consideration. The subject may well parry a baton strike with his or her weak arm then lunge towards at the officer before he or she can recover and strike the subject again.

Due to the speed of a knife attack, unless the officer's baton has already been drawn, there is unlikely to be the time available to use it. Empty handed techniques are a last resort and should only be used in self-defence when no other option is available. Nevertheless officers should be trained in empty handed techniques to protect themselves from an unexpected knife attack.

Someone wielding a club, baseball bat, pool cue or chair leg is also a serious threat to officer survival. Adopt the 'CUT' immediate action.

SUMMARY

Consider the following:

I Being concealed from view does not automatically mean officers are safe from gunfire. Officers need to know what does, and does not, constitute bullet proof cover.

I Think 'cover' whenever approaching an incident.

I Know the 'Six Cs' immediate action when attending a firearms incident.

I Treat anyone with an edged weapon as 'high risk' whatever their age, gender, strength or skill.

I Know and practice the 'CUT' immediate action for dealing with an edged weapon threat.

Chapter eleven

FIRST AID/SELF AID

KEYPOINTS

Use this chapter to find out:

I *What emergency aid is.*

I *How to perform cardio-pulmonary resuscitation (CPR).*

I *How to treat wounds.*

I *How to recognise and treat shock.*

I *What threat is posed by body fluids.*

Chapter eleven

First Aid/Self Aid

However much operational dangers are reduced it is almost, inevitable that police officers will suffer injuries, especially in unexpected attacks. It is one of the sad facts of life that officers have a unique occupation, although some people may be injured or killed whilst engaged in their work, eg, miners, officers face injury or death because of the job they do and what they represent to some people. Although murders on duty are mercifully rare it is the malice with which they are carried out which is disturbing.

Be ready to deal with trauma, that is the effects of knife or gunshot wounds. Two of the biggest killers of police officers happen to be heart attacks and road accidents. Good first aid and self-aid is of paramount importance. Officers must not become complacent and hope that because they work in an urban area an ambulance will only be a few minutes away. A severed artery can produce unconsciousness in as little as a few seconds and death in a couple of minutes.

The aims of first aid are:

I To save life.

I To prevent the casualty's condition from deteriorating.

In the crudest terms, officers must ensure that the medical team at the accident and emergency unit have a live casualty to treat. The most valuable thing officers may ever have to do for their colleagues is to keep them alive until they are in the hands of the paramedics. It is vital that officers take any opportunity to attend first aid training to keep their skills up to date. The writer recommends that all police officers at least obtain the latest first aid manual to refresh their memories. This chapter is designed specifically for the operational officer at the sharp end of giving first aid.

EMERGENCY AID

The worst case scenario for police officers would be the need to give life saving first aid to colleagues whilst a serious threat to their safety is still present, such as an individual brandishing a weapon. Officers need to assess the incident and identify the risks to themselves and the casualty. Make the area safe for the casualty and summon help.

In this situation the officer has to protect the casualty and himself from further injury. A natural reaction may well be anger directed against the individual and a desire to overpower him immediately. The assailant has

The first priority is to protect injured colleagues from further injury.

shown himself capable of injuring a colleague and he can probably injure another officer. Instead of trying to overpower the assailant it may be better to:

▌ Get an obstacle in between the officer and the attacker.

▌ Get distance between the officer and the attacker. Keep that distance by verbal commands and baton techniques.

▌ Get backup, properly equipped and trained to contain the attacker.

▌ Get an ambulance.

ASSESSING THE CASUALTY

Once the scene is safe assess the casualty's condition using the DR ABC procedure.

▌ DANGER – Assess danger to yourself and the casualty.

▌ RESPONSE – Check consciousness level.

▌ AIRWAY – Check the airway.

▌ BREATHING – Check for breathing.

▌ CIRCULATION – Check for a pulse.

Any First Aid training must be done under the guidance of a qualified first aid trainer. Techniques such as cardio-pulmonary resuscitation must only be practised on training aids.

TREATMENT OF THE CASUALTY

Conscious	Breathing	Pulse	Treatment
No	No	No	1. Call for ambulance. 2. Commence CPR.
No	No	Yes	1. Ten ventilations. 2. Call for ambulance. 3. Continue ventilations.
No	Yes	Yes	1. Treat serious injury and place in recovery position. 2. Call for ambulance.
Yes	Yes	Yes	1. Treat injuries. 2. Call for ambulance if required.

Checking Level of Consciousness

Question and command technique:

I 'Can you hear me?'

I 'Open your eyes!'

I Carefully shake the casualty's shoulders.

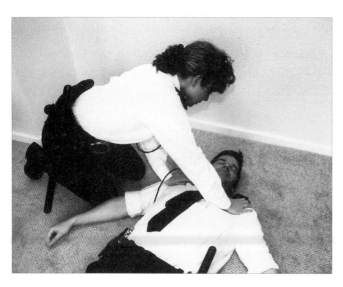

Ask a question, give a command and shake the casualty's shoulders.

Checking the Airway

Clear the mouth of any obstructions. Look inside and sweep out debris using two fingers. Loosen clothing at the neck. Lift the jaw by using two fingers under the chin and tilt the head back placing a hand on the casualty's forehead.

Checking Breathing

The aider places the side of her face near the casualty's mouth:

I LOOK – For rise and fall of the chest.

I LISTEN – For any breathing.

I FEEL – For any exhaled air on her cheek.

Checking Circulation

Check for a pulse at the carotid arteries which lie either side of the Adam's apple.

I The aider locates the Adam's apple and slides her fingers into the depression between the muscles in the neck and the Adam's apple.

I She checks for five seconds before concluding that there is no pulse present.

Clear the airway by sweeping the casualty's mouth and tilting his head.

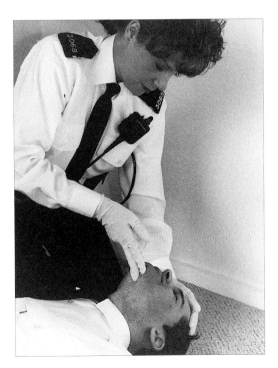

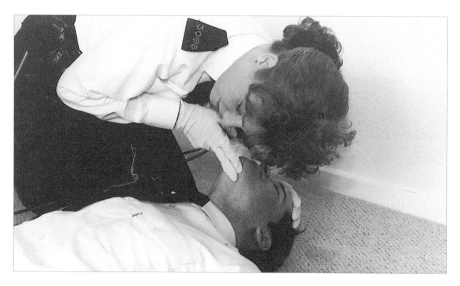

Look, listen and feel for breathing.

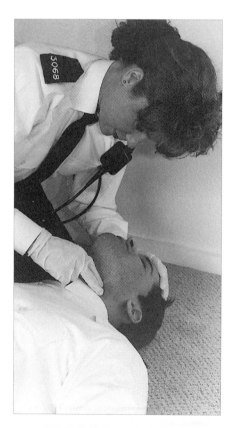

Check the carotid pulse.

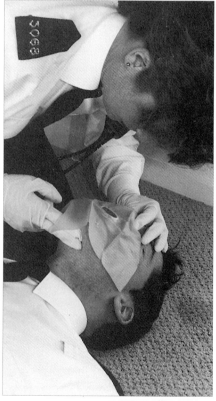

With a face shield in place the aider commences resuscitation.

142

CARDIO-PULMONARY RESUSCITATION (CPR)

Casualties who are not breathing require a first aider to breathe oxygen into their bodies. The amount of oxygen in a person's exhaled breath is sufficient to resuscitate a casualty. Be mindful of protection from disease whilst giving resuscitation and use a face shield. Due to the urgency of the need to give resuscitation it should not be delayed if a first aider does not have a face shield.

Procedure

Clear the airway. Lie the casualty on his back. Clear any debris from the casualty's mouth.

Open the airway. Tilt the casualty's head back and lift the chin.

The aider seals the casualty's nose by pinching it with her finger and thumb, she takes a deep breath and seals her mouth over his mouth. The aider blows hard enough until she see the casualty's chest rise.

The aider removes her mouth and, when the casualty's chest has fallen fully, continue resuscitation at a rate of approximately 10 breaths per minute. She checks the pulse for five seconds at the carotid artery after every ten breaths. If there is no pulse she continues CPR.

If the chest does not rise it may mean that either:

▮ she has not tilted the casualty's head back far enough to open the airway, or

▮ she has not sealed the casualty's mouth properly, or

▮ she has not closed the casualty's nose properly, or

▮ there is an obstruction in the airway.

Clearing an obstructed airway

First, the aider re-checks the casualty's mouth for any debris. She does this by turning his head to one side; opening his mouth and sweeping two fingers around to hook out any matter.

If these procedures fail to clear the obstruction use backslaps or abdominal thrusts.

Backslaps

Kneeling beside the casualty the aider rolls him over towards her and support his chest against her knees.

With the flat of her hand the aider gives the casualty five sharp slaps between his shoulder blades.

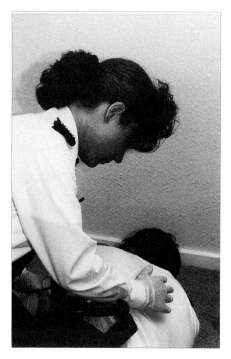

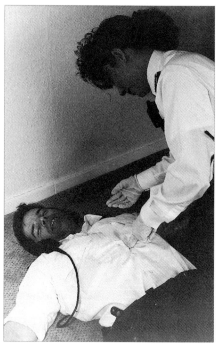

Backslaps may clear an obstructed airway.

The aider locates the bottom of the sternum.

Abdominal thrusts

If backslaps do not clear the obstruction the aider turns the casualty onto his back and tilts his head back. She kneels astride the casualty and, with one hand on top of the other, thrusts hard inwards and upwards beneath the rib cage. She repeats this up to five times to clear the airway.

CPR

If the heart stops then the brain will be deprived of oxygenated blood. Therefore the aider must oxygenate the blood by mouth to mouth ventilation and also pump the blood around the body by chest compressions. This can be done by one aider, but is most effective if two people are doing it.

The casualty must be lying on his back on a hard surface. The aider kneels beside the casualty and locates the bottom of the sternum (breastbone) by running two fingers along the lowest rib to where it joins the sternum in the middle. The aider places two fingers on the lowest part of the sternum.

The aider then places the heel of one hand on the sternum above the two fingers of her other hand. This is the correct point to apply compression.

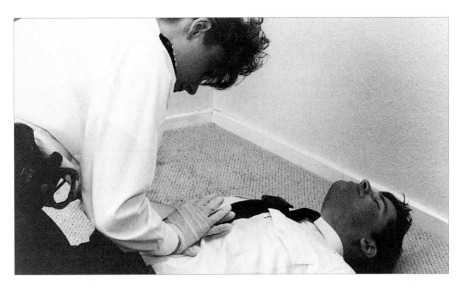

Abdominal thrusts may clear an obstructed airway.

Interlock the fingers and keep them away from the rib cage.

The aider then presses down vertically on the sternum about 4 to 5 cm before releasing pressure. This is repeated at a rate of 80 compressions per minute. It is important to keep the arms straight by locking the elbows out and to keep directly above the casualty to prevent rocking the rib cage.

This must be combined with mouth to mouth to have any effect. If the aider is on her own she should perform **two inflations to every fifteen compressions**. If there are two aiders working on the casualty they should perform **one inflation to every five compressions**.

The Recovery Position

If the casualty is unconscious, but his breathing and circulation are all right move him into the recovery position. This will ensure that the airway remains open. The airway may become blocked if a casualty is left lying on his back due to the tongue dropping back or him choking on his vomit.

The aider removes the equipment belt from the casualty before she moves him. Kneeling next to the casualty and making sure his airway is open by tilting his head well back, the aider bends the casualty's arm closest to her to 90 degrees with the palm up.

Next, the aider moves the casualty's other arm towards her and holds the back of his hand against the side of his face nearest to her.

Finally, the aider bends the casualty's leg furthest away from her so that

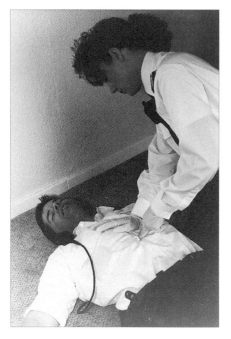

The aider places the heel of her hand on the sternum and interlocks her fingers.

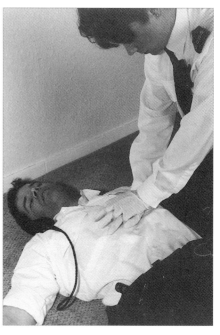

Keeping her arms locked straight the aider compresses the casualty's chest.

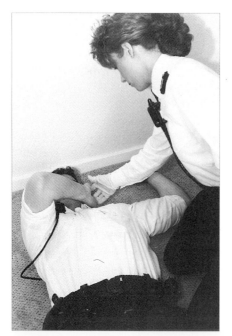

Getting ready to move the casualty into the recovery position.

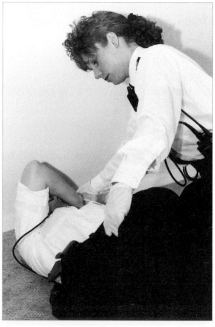

Protecting the casualty's face with his own hand.

Placing the casualty in the recovery position.

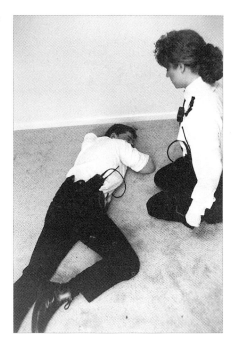

his foot is flat on the floor. Keeping a grip of the casualty's leg above the knee she pulls him over towards her knees whilst keeping his hand against his face.

The aider ensures that the casualty's head is tilted well back to keep his airway open and she moves the bent leg to a right angle.

The aider monitors the breathing and pulse of the casualty regularly.

WOUND TREATMENT

One major effect of a gunshot or knife wound is the severing of a major blood vessel especially an artery. Arteries carry bright red oxygenated blood from the heart under pressure. If an artery is severed the blood will spurt out and if emergency aid is not given quickly the casualty may well die. In the worst cases of a severed artery unconsciousness can occur in a few seconds and death in a minute or so. There is a small window of opportunity to stem the flow of blood and keep the casualty alive. It is essential officers do something rather than praying for the ambulance to hurry up. Often casualties will not know immediately that they have been stabbed or shot. If officers realise that they have been wounded they are, by definition, conscious – this is a good sign. Officers therefore have a fighting chance of survival.

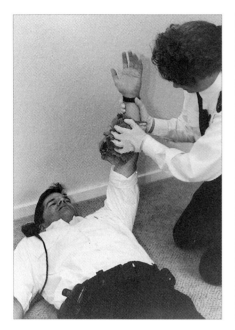

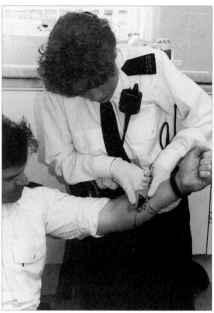

Use a sterile dressing, apply direct pressure to a wound and elevate the limb if possible.

Apply pressure either side of a wound containing a foreign object, eg, a piece of broken glass.

Treatment for External Bleeding

Uncover the wound site. Rip away any clothing from the wound. Beware of sharps which may cause harm, such as shards of glass.

Compress the wound site with a sterile dressing if available. If no sterile dressing is available officers must improvise or even use their hands. Keep the pressure applied for 10 minutes or more to permit the clotting action of the blood to start.

Officers may have to compress the area around the wound site if there is a foreign body, such as glass, protruding from the wound.

Get the limb elevated and supported above the level of the casualty's heart. This will reduce the blood pressure at the wound site. Lie the casualty down to minimise blood loss and reduce the effects of shock.

Apply a sterile dressing to the wound. Should blood seep through the first dressing do not remove it, but apply further dressings on top.

If officers cannot stop the bleeding by direct pressure they should apply pressure to a 'pressure point'. Namely the brachial artery in the upper arm or the femoral pressure point in the groin. The pressure must not be maintained for more than 15 minutes. Do not apply a tourniquet.

Treat for shock.

Treatment for Internal Bleeding

Although not as visually shocking, internal bleeding can, and does, kill. Internal bleeding could be caused by a gunshot wound or from receiving a severe kicking causing damage to internal organs, such as the spleen.

The blood lost from the internal organs needs replacing with blood of the same type as the casualty's, ideally at body temperature. In fact if the casualty's legs are raised the blood in their legs will drain to their body and will provide a perfect transfusion.

Lie the casualty down and raise his legs.

Loosen the casualty's clothing, especially at the neck and waist. Monitor his pulse and level of consciousness. Should the casualty become unconscious move him into the recovery position.

Treat for shock.

Penetrating Chest Injury

A penetrating chest injury is caused by an instrument, such as an edged weapon, penetrating the rib cage and perforating the membranes surrounding the lungs. As air enters the chest the lungs collapse. As well as injury to internal organs, especially the heart, the casualty will experience difficulty in breathing.

At the wound site the blood will bubble out and there may be a sucking noise as air enters the chest.

The first priority is to form an airtight seal over the wound. Get the casualty, if he is conscious, to cover the wound with his hand.

Apply a sterile wound dressing to the wound and an airtight cover, such as a plastic bag. Secure the airtight cover with tape.

Prop the casualty up and lean him over towards the injured side. This will prevent any blood from the injured lung from entering the uninjured one. Get medical assistance quickly.

Treat for shock.

If the casualty is unconscious – place in the recovery position and resuscitate if required.

SHOCK

Shock is a medical condition caused by a loss of blood from the system. This can be caused for example by severe bleeding or a heart attack.

Shock must be treated quickly. Shock can kill as the vital organs, especially the heart, fail.

149

Signs and Symptoms of Shock

I A fast, weak pulse leading to an irregular pulse.

I Pale clammy skin.

I Fast, shallow breathing leading to gasping for air.

I Complaint of weakness, nausea, thirst and feeling faint.

The casualty will become unconscious and die unless treated and given medical attention quickly.

Treatment for Shock

First of all apply treatment to any cause of shock, such as severe bleeding, then lay the casualty flat. Raise his legs and support them to improve blood supply to the body.

Keep the casualty warm and loosen restrictive clothing, such as the equipment belt. Call for assistance.

Moisten the casualty's lips with water, but do not give him anything to eat or drink.

It is crucial to stay with the casualty until help arrives. **Constantly reassure the casualty**.

Keep monitoring the pulse and breathing. If necessary the aider may have to resuscitate the casualty.

SELF-AID

The same first aid principles apply to an officer who is without assistance when wounded. It is important for the officer to realise that there may be only a matter of minutes between the realisation that he or she has been wounded until unconsciousness prevails.

I Apply direct pressure to wounds to slow the rate of blood loss.

I Lie down and prevent fainting by keeping your head low and your legs raised, if possible.

I Ease your breathing by loosening clothing at the waist and neck.

I Keep yourself warm.

I Summon medical help.

I Control your breathing by slow deep breaths. Tell yourself that you will survive.

BODY FLUID THREAT

The Occupational Health Units will give officers advice on the threat to their health from body fluid contamination.

There are two main threats from body fluids, namely Hepatitis B and Human Immunodeficiency Virus (HIV).

Hepatitis B is a virus carried in blood which affects the liver. It is only fatal in a small proportion of people contracting this disease. It is extremely infectious; only a small amount of infected body fluid, eg, blood, can cause Hepatitis B.

Most people with HIV eventually develop the Acquired Immune Deficiency Syndrome (AIDS) for which there is as yet no known cure. It is usually transmitted by the transfer of body fluids, eg:

▮ Unprotected sex.

▮ The sharing of needles.

▮ Inherited by a baby from its mother.

Operational Measures

It is not worth being complacent about Hepatitis B or HIV. When dealing with others sensible precautions must always be taken to reduce the risk of being infected by contaminated body fluids.

▮ Ensure your Hepatitis B vaccination is current. If not arrange a blood test or booster with your GP.

▮ Cover any broken skin with a waterproof plaster.

▮ Always carry a personal protection kit on you whilst on duty. The kit should contain disposable protective gloves, medical wipes, a face shield and a waste bag.

▮ Ensure your police vehicle has a properly equipped first aid kit and blood spillage pack.

▮ Where there is a likelihood of encountering body fluids, eg, an injury accident or when assisting in the taking of samples, wear disposable protective gloves.

▮ Practice safe searching techniques of persons, vehicles and premises to prevent injury from sharps.

▮ Dispose of contaminated waste safely.

▮ Decontaminate clothing and equipment, eg, handcuffs, which have been affected by body fluids. Familiarise yourself with your force's instructions regarding the appropriate decontamination routines.

SUMMARY

It is essential for police officers to preserve the lives of their colleagues.

Make the effort to benefit from any first aid training which is available.

Take precautions to minimise the risk posed by body fluid contamination.

RECOMMENDED READING

St John Ambulance/St Andrews Ambulance/British Red Cross First Aid Manuals.

Chapter twelve

SURVIVAL OF THE FITTEST

KEYPOINTS

Use this chapter to find out:

I *What are the essential elements of physical fitness for police officers.*

I *What is the criterion for a precautionary medical examination.*

I *How officers should assess their current fitness level.*

I *What are the elements of warm-up, stretching and cool-down routines.*

I *Which fitness programme is most suitable for the individual.*

Chapter twelve

Survival of the Fittest

FITNESS AND THE POLICE OFFICER

Research indicates that the public at large are becoming less fit. Fewer than three men and one woman in twenty take part in regular weekly exercise. Almost half of the population are overweight. Britons watch, on average, 25 hours of television per week.

As police officers are drawn from society it is not surprising that corresponding developments in their fitness can be observed. Although there are many officers who are physically very fit, the majority are of average fitness. This is likely to remain so unless mandatory fitness tests are introduced. If the reader's level of fitness has declined in the years since leaving training school, he or she is not alone. As the years go by humans tend to lose fitness and gain weight.

Patrol work often means sedentary activities such as driving, report writing and interviewing. Shift work is also not healthy for individuals since it often means eating and drinking at odd hours of the day. The stress of operational policework can have officers reaching for the cigarettes, a bottle of beer or the biscuit tin.

There are only occasional physical demands in patrol work, for example chasing and restraining a violent prisoner or dispersing a crowd. Patrol work in itself is not a physical job like labouring, there is virtually no

Chasing a suspect on foot is a severe test of speed, stamina and strength.

measurable degree of physical activity in police work. If the work will not ensure that officers keep a minimum level of fitness they need to do something about it themselves. The organisation may assist or encourage police officers to get fitter, but ultimately every officer must take responsibility, as a professional, for his or her own fitness.

ADVANTAGES OF FITNESS

Having realised the need for improved fitness officers can take encouragement from the added advantages of becoming fitter. Some of the advantages of physical fitness are:

I You will be more motivated.

I You may cope with stress better.

I You are likely to feel better.

I Your sleep will improve.

I Your joints and muscles will be in better condition.

I Your circulation will improve.

I Your weight may reduce to your ideal target weight.

I Your blood pressure should reduce to a normal level.

I You will have a stronger heart.

I Your cholesterol levels may reduce.

Of course there are disadvantages to anything. Becoming fitter has the following drawbacks:

I It will cost money; the purchase of appropriate training shoes and sports clothes, maybe even a bicycle or a subscription to a leisure club or attending a swimming pool or gym.

I It will consume time. Other leisure pursuits may have to be cut back. A fitness programme may mean giving up several hours of watching television each week.

I It will need personal commitment. Officers will need motivation to undertake physical activity. When going out jogging the most difficult step is that first one.

Police officers at the 'sharp end' should never view physical fitness as an optional extra. Attaining and keeping physical fitness is difficult and expensive in terms of time and money, but officers can consider it an investment which will benefit their career and quality of life. Those who do not care about their fitness would do well to consider the following quotation:

'And he that will his health deny.
Down among the dead men let him lie.'

John Dyer (18th Century)

THE ELEMENTS OF FITNESS

To survive a physical confrontation in an operational policing environment officers need four elements of personal fitness:

- **I** MUSCULAR STRENGTH – This is particularly important in the upper body. A good test of upper body strength is the ability of officers to lift themselves above their own shoulder height in order to cross obstacles, such as walls. This type of strength will help officers overpower another person should the conflict lead to physical contact. Although equipment, such as batons and rigid handcuffs, can assist in restraining another person, strength is required to apply these techniques. The spin-off from good upper body strength is the improvement in posture and therefore some protection from back injury.

- **I** MUSCULAR STAMINA – Stamina is essential in order to keep going in a physical confrontation for longer than an opponent. If officers start to become fatigued before their opponents do, they are in trouble. To sprint after and catch a violent subject is a very severe test of stamina, so muscles need to be conditioned by exercise to endure repeated demands on them. Muscular strength and stamina are improved by a regular exercise regime.

- **I** CARDIOVASCULAR ENDURANCE – This is the amount of physical activity a body can cope with. Efficient heart, lungs and blood supply are crucial if the muscles are to be provided with the oxygen they need. This is probably the most important part of fitness and is improved by aerobic activity, such as jogging, swimming and cycling.

- **I** SUPPLENESS – This is the flexibility to reduce the risk of injury whilst performing physical activity. Officers maintain suppleness through stretching exercises so that each joint keeps its full range of movement.

PRECAUTIONARY MEDICAL EXAMINATION

Before embarking on a physical training regime readers must be sensible. It is going to take time to achieve even a modest improvement in fitness. Officers should obtain a medical examination if they fall within **any** of the following criteria:

- **I** you are over 30 years of age, or

- **I** you are overweight, or

- **I** you have ever had heart trouble or other cardiovascular problems, such as high blood pressure, or

I you have a family history of heart disease, or

I you are a heavy smoker, or

I you experience chest pains after exerting yourself, or

I you often experience headaches, dizziness or feeling faint, or

I you have a painful joint, for example knee damage due to an old sports injury, which is made worse by exercise, or

I you are on medication or getting over an operation, or

I you have any medical concerns which may affect your participation in a physical fitness programme.

If readers fit into **any** of the above criteria please consult a medical professional before embarking on a physical fitness programme. Occupational Health Units will be able to advise officers on the procedure for arranging a medical examination.

When exercising, officers may inevitably pick up a cold or influenza at some time. Vigorous exercise whilst suffering from the symptoms of a cold or the 'flu can be hazardous to the heart. It is therefore vital to rest until clear of the virus.

Likewise, if officers sustain an injury – stop exercising.

Once officers have had a precautionary medical examination they will be ready to embark on a physical fitness programme. As with any journey officers need to know where they are now and where they want to get to. A good start is a physical fitness assessment.

PHYSICAL FITNESS ASSESSMENT

A physical fitness assessment will measure officers' current fitness level, so they can then identify a realistic goal for themselves. This assessment is best administered by a professional; some leisure clubs and centres offer this type of assessment. The leisure centre staff will also advise officers on the most appropriate forms of training for them to reach their goal. A re-assessment will give officers an indication of their progress.

There are many types of fitness assessment which officers can administer themselves. These assessments usually measure static exercises, such as push-ups and sit-ups, and a timed run. Readers can find these types of assessments in the two books recommended at the end of this chapter.

Police officers applying to be authorised firearms officers (AFOs) must undergo a similar type of fitness assessment. The details of the AFO fitness test can be found in the *Manual of Guidance on the Police Use of Firearms*.

Upper Body Strength

This is usually measured by the total number of push-ups for male officers and knee press-ups for female officers completed within one minute. Officers start in the supported position, ie, arms straight. An officer may take only one rest in the front supported position, ie, with the arms fully extended, for no more than five seconds.

For a male officer the weight must be borne on his hands and feet. His body must be kept straight with his hands shoulder width apart. He must make contact with a fist sized object directly beneath his chest each time he dips.

To minimise the risk of strain to internal organs female officers should adopt the knee push-up position. The weight is borne on the hands and knees and the forehead must touch the floor on each dip. The body must be kept in a straight line from the knee to the head.

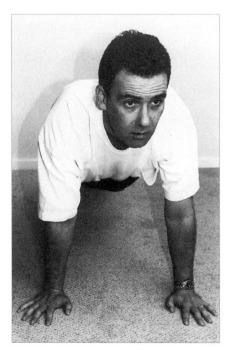 

Male push-ups.   *Female push-ups.*

Abdominal Strength

This is measured by the total number of completed sit-ups in one minute.

Officers start by lying on their back, feet held flat on the floor and their arms folded across their chest. As the officer sits up he touches his knees with his forearms and returns to the start position.

Sit-ups

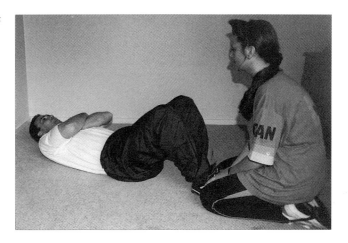

For a fuller explanation of the test and the scoring table officers should consult the *Manual of Guidance for the Police Use of Firearms*, if they have access to it. The test must be conducted by a qualified PE trainer.

Tests similar to this are becoming more common in selecting officers for specialist units, such as public order units.

It could be argued that this type of test is applicable to all operational police officers. In an organisation which can ill-afford to have officers abstracted from their duty to undertake fitness training, some creative way could be sought to motivate all officers sufficiently to train in their own time to pass the above test.

THE WARM-UP, STRETCHING AND COOL-DOWN ROUTINES

To minimise the risk of injury and to improve suppleness it is essential to do warm-up and stretching routines before each session of physical train-ing. To reduce the discomfort of sore muscles which contract too fast after exercise it is also important to go through a cool-down routine at the end of each session.

The warm-up consists of light exercises designed to mobilise all the joints in the body from top to toe. These get the blood pumping to the major muscle groups and allow free movement of the joints. A brisk five minutes of pedalling on an exercise bicycle is one example of a good warm-up exercise.

Stretching exercises must be done slowly. As each position is adopted it should be held for between 10 and 15 seconds before being slowly released. Ballistic stretching, ie, bouncing to stretch a muscle group, can cause injury and should be avoided.

Cool-down exercises are simply a repetition of the warm-up mobility exercises and the stretching exercises. Although they are simple they should not be ignored or the muscles and joints may suffer unnecessary soreness due to a sudden cessation of physical activity.

Books devoted to fitness give detailed instructions on all types of warm-up, stretching and cool-down exercises. Try them out and establish a suitable routine.

Officers will now be ready to undertake some physical activity.

FITNESS PROGRAMMES

By this stage officers will be medically sound to undertake a fitness programme and their current state of fitness will have been assessed. Now what?

The fitness programme officers are going to follow will have the following characteristics:

I It must be balanced to improve strength, stamina, endurance and suppleness.

I It must include aerobic activity, such as swimming.

I It must include resistance activity, such as working against weights.

I It must be done regularly, say three or four times per week.

I It must include rest days if very intense activity is carried out to restore the body's energy reserves.

I It must increase the workload progressively as an individual's fitness improves, without leading to exhaustion.

I **It needs to be interesting and enjoyable with variety**.

The exercise must be right for the officer, fitting in with his or her shift patterns and be accessible (and affordable).

Some examples of exercises are:

I Fast walking (so called 'power walking')

I Jogging or running

I Cycling

I Swimming

I Team sports

I Tennis or squash

I Circuit training, aerobics or step classes

It might be a combination of activities such as aerobic work on cycling and rowing machines together with multi-gym exercises followed by a swim.

Whatever programme is undertaken, it needs to be done regularly, improvements should be monitored, and, it has to be enjoyable! After all it has got to be better than paperwork!

NUTRITION

No chapter on fitness would be complete without a mention of nutrition. To improve officers' health they must monitor what they eat. If individuals consume more energy (calories) than they expend they will store it as fat.

The following general dietary advice should have a positive impact on most peoples' health.

I Each day eat three balanced meals, including fresh fruit and vegetables.

I Cut down on fat consumption, especially saturated fats.

I Monitor your cholesterol level.

I Reduce salt intake.

I Increase fibre intake.

Occupational Health Units can give dietary advice including alcohol intake and giving up smoking.

SUMMARY

Thirty years in an abrasive occupation like the police service can, quite simply, wear people out. Achieving fitness can assist officers' long-term health as well as improving performance immediately in the policework officers are engaged in.

By adopting a healthy lifestyle and fitness programme police officers will be laying the foundations for a long and healthy retirement. The job will appreciate officers being fitter now; their families and friends will appreciate them living a longer and healthier life.

FURTHER READING

R Hoffman and TR Collingwood (1995) *Fit for Duty*, Human Kinetics, Illinois.

R Eggar (1993) *The Royal Marines Total Fitness*, Vermilion, London.

Chapter thirteen

DANGEROUS STREETS

KEYPOINTS

Use this chapter to find out:

I *What factors are associated with assaults on police officers.*

I *Why there is no such thing as 'low risk' in officer survival.*

I *How good communication skills can diffuse confrontational situations.*

I *The need to remain alert throughout the search, arrest and escort phases.*

I *The importance of maintaining a safe distance between police officers and potential assailants.*

Chapter thirteen

Dangerous Streets

ASSAULTS ON POLICE

Thankfully the incidence of fatal assaults upon police officers in Britain is rare. Operational police officers however should take no comfort in this, a recent research study has found that nearly two out of every three constables on patrol duties had been assaulted in the previous 12 months. The only acceptable level of assaults on police officers is nil.

This section highlights which officers are most likely to be assaulted, who commits the assaults, and the circumstances in which these assaults occur.

The writer has analysed more than 500 police assault reports in Cheshire over a three year period and these have been compared with other studies into police assaults in this country and abroad.

Several research studies on police assaults have arrived at similar conclusions which suggests that the characteristics of the officer, the offender, and the circumstances, involved in police assaults are consistent. It can therefore be predicted which incidents are statistically more likely to result in an assault on police, taking into consideration such factors as location, time of day, day of the week, and offender profile. Armed with this knowledge the reader can intelligently assess the dangers in any incident on the street.

There are two important considerations to be always borne in mind:

I Firstly, be safety conscious whatever the situation. Just because the circumstances do not appear to contain high risk factors does not mean that it is a safe situation. An elderly shoplifter may be so distraught about the adverse consequences of being arrested and possibly taken to court that he or she may view assaulting an officer in order to escape as the only option. There is 'high risk' and 'unknown risk', operational police officers can never be confident enough to classify any situation as 'low risk'.

I Secondly, in 'high risk' situations be even more aware of safety, but just because high risk factors are recognised it does not mean that it is inevitable that police officers will be assaulted. If police officers conclude that they will **always** be assaulted in such circumstances, they will naturally adopt an aggressive approach. Research has shown (Wilson, 1993) that those officers who adopt an aggressive approach face more resistance from the public and therefore increase their chances of being assaulted.

POLICE OFFICERS

Constables (89%), and to a lesser extent sergeants (9%) and inspectors (2%), engaged in operational duties are at the greatest risk of being assaulted. They tend to be under 30 years of age with an average length of service of almost 8 years. These officers are most likely to be found performing patrol duty. This is not a criticism of junior officers, but reflects the fact that these officers are more likely to be found on patrol and therefore more likely to be assaulted.

The majority (85%) of officers assaulted are male. This correlates to the proportion of male and female officers employed on operational duty. Gender does not appear to be a factor in whether an officer is assaulted or not. Chivalry is dead when it comes to assaulting police officers.

Nine out of ten officers assaulted are from the uniform department, motorway and motor patrol (traffic). Only 3% are CID officers, reflecting the fact that it is the uniformed officer who polices the streets at the peak times for the commission of these offences. Another study found that officers engaged on uniform patrol accounted for 78% of those assaulted (Brown, 1994).

Other research studies have identified that a small proportion of officers are assaulted significantly more often than the rest. One study (Wilson, 1993) found that some officers experienced increased resistance from subjects they were dealing with. This significant difference cannot be explained by demographic factors, such as age, department and length of service. It seems therefore that unconsciously, or otherwise, some officers attract resistance from other people.

ASSAILANTS

In Cheshire 85% of assailants were male. The average age for all assailants was 26 years. This was slightly older than other studies. The age range started in the first year of secondary school (12 years old), right through to pensionable age (66 years old).

In half the incidents in Cheshire the offender was accompanied by at least one other associate. Other research (Christopher & Noakes, 1989) indicated that the assailant was likely to receive encouragement to assault police officers from his or her friends. The same study also found that assailants harboured aggressive tendencies against anyone in positions of authority. In their interviews with assailants they found that the assailant's recourse to violence was not exceptional behaviour for them.

In the same study Christopher & Noakes also found that in some 40% of cases the assailants actually knew the officer they had assaulted. Therefore saying, 'It's OK. I've dealt with Jimmy Smith in the past. I'll take him in without handcuffs', may be an officer's epitaph.

Another significant finding from the above study is that the assailant perceived the officer to be 'arrogant'. Readers could be defensive about this perception from the offender, 'The assailant would say that wouldn't he?' However this issue does need addressing. Even if officers are not arrogant they may be perceived as acting arrogantly. Efforts should be made to reduce this misconception by modifying communication both verbally and non-verbally and acting with empathy.

Drink was recorded as a contributory factor in two out of three assaults on police officers in the Cheshire study. Other studies have also found that alcohol consumption is a common denominator in many of the assaults on police officers. Although many assailants are intoxicated when they assault police officers; many, many more people become intoxicated without assaulting police officers. It is not possible therefore to state that alcohol consumption causes people to assault police officers. Instead alcohol may be the gunpowder waiting for a spark to trigger an explosion.

Drugs were recorded as a contributory factor in one in five assaults in Cheshire. These recordings were subjective in that they were made by the assaulted officer. It may be that there is under or over reporting of the influence of substances. An offender could well be affected by the consumption of drugs of which the police officer was unaware.

A recipe for disaster?

CIRCUMSTANCES OF ASSAULT

In Cheshire most assaults occur in public places, especially town centres. Ten per cent to 20% occurred in or close to licensed premises (pubs and night-clubs) especially around closing time.

The peak period for assaults appears to be from 9 pm to 4 am, especially at weekends. Afternoon and evening periods are the next most risky period for assaults.

In most assaults the officer had the opportunity of communicating with the offender, so it would appear that the officer's communication skills were not sufficient to prevent an assault. In some situations the subject may be so irrational, due to the influence of drink, drugs, mental illness or emotional anger that, however skilled officers are, they cannot prevent the subject trying to launch an assault. Most people can be 'talked down' or 'wound up' by the use, or misuse, of communication. Endeavours must be made to improve communication skills.

Between a quarter and a third of assaults occur after the arrest, either when being transported or when in the police station. This could be due to officers 'switching off' once the arrest is over, resulting in lax prisoner handling. There is a need constantly to improve skills in escorting prisoners from the point of arrest, transporting them in police vehicles, and throughout the entire custody procedure.

The provision of data on the circumstances of assaults on police could lull officers into a mindset that it is only young drunk males at closing time who commit assaults. The data should however give officers fair warning regarding the likelihood of assaults taking place at certain times and certain locations. From an organisational perspective this information can be used by deploying more double-crewed vehicles and vans at the peak times for police assaults. These statistics should not be seen as some infallible criteria for assessing the risk of assault in a given situation. There is never a 'low risk' situation when it comes to officer safety.

Mercifully it is only a minority of assaults (17%) which are severe, for example fractures and serious wounds (Brown, 1994). The vast majority (93%) in Cheshire were caused by punches, kicks or headbutts. Only a small percentage were caused by weapons. If a safe distance can be kept between the officer and the subject the chance of being assaulted can be greatly reduced. This safe distance (reactionary gap) is lost in two ways:

I the subject moves towards the police officer, possibly intending to assault him or her, or

I the police officer moves towards the subject to search and/or arrest.

The most serious assaults occurred when officers interrupted offences in progress, ie, catching a criminal 'red-handed'. In these situations the assailant would be motivated to escape being arrested at all costs. The assailants used any weapons they had with them or picked up anything lying around. These spontaneous incidents were the most hazardous for operational police officers.

Traffic stops are also hazardous for police officers. The assailant may use the vehicle as a weapon by driving it at officers and he may use articles from the vehicle as weapons, such as a wheel brace. It is often a passenger in the vehicle, rather than the driver, who commits the assault.

Domestic disputes are an obvious source of danger, most murders stem from domestic disputes. Officers intervene in what can be a very volatile situation in an environment full of potential dangers, for example a kitchen drawer full of knives. It is important to assess disputes and control the risks by keeping the parties away from hazards, such as improvised weapons.

When police officers are at close quarters with an individual they must employ tactics and self-defence techniques to engage the person to ensure the safety of all concerned.

ROAD TRAFFIC ACCIDENTS

Police officers involved in pursuits are many times more likely to be involved in an accident than during a routine patrol. This likelihood has been calculated as **more than one thousand times more dangerous than routine patrol** (Alpert & Dunham, 1990).

Response driving (driving to an emergency) is also far more dangerous than routine patrol driving. Speeds are increased, time to react and margins for error are reduced.

Routine patrol and off-duty driving accidents also account for deaths and injuries to police officers.

Taken as a whole driving accidents account for far more police fatalities than do assaults. If police officers can improve their defensive driving techniques they should be able to reduce the risk involved in all types of driving conditions.

SUMMARY

Consider the following:

I The need to recognise the factors involved in police assaults.

I There is no such category as 'low risk' – only 'high risk' or 'unknown risk'.

I The importance of keeping a safe distance, good communication, and effective close quarter techniques.

I The need for defensive driving techniques.

Chapter fourteen

POLICE DRIVING

KEYPOINTS

Use this chapter to find out:

I *How to conduct a pre-patrol vehicle inspection.*

I *Safety factors when on routine patrol.*

I *What are the guidelines involved in response and pursuit driving.*

Chapter fourteen

Police Driving

INTRODUCTION

In the last few years as many police officers have been killed in pursuit accidents as have died as a result of being assaulted. If the deaths whilst driving to an emergency (response driving) and those whilst engaged in routine patrol driving are added it is easy to see that there is a need to review police driving.

Police patrol driving is **not** all about fast driving. No organisation can afford to lose resources, such as police officers or vehicles. Each officer lost is a human tragedy. There is also not an unlimited stock of vehicles from which officers can obtain 'remounts'. Today's patrol vehicles are required tomorrow and the day after – losing patrol vehicles by rash driving has dire consequences for the organisation.

PRE-PATROL INSPECTION

However much the public hanker after foot patrols when they telephone they want a patrol car to attend promptly; vehicles are therefore essential for policing today's society.

Police officers must ensure that the patrol vehicles they use are in good order. Experience shows that the best kept vehicles are those 'adopted' by the same personnel, eg, traffic units, dog handlers and rural beat officers. These officers take on a responsibility for their vehicles which is missing when patrol vehicles are drawn from a pool.

Prior to taking patrol vehicles onto the road officers need to inspect them visually, concentrating on those matters which are particularly important to safety:

I Check tyres, tread and pressure.

I Check that child locks are on the rear doors.

I Check the rear compartment for weapons or contraband, lift the rear seat and look underneath the front seats.

Other checks, such as oil and coolant levels, should be done, but do not impact on officer safety as much as the above measures.

Once officers are satisfied with the checks they should conduct the cockpit drill.

Before taking vehicles on the road consider their characteristics which will affect performance:

- Front or rear wheel drive?

- Petrol or diesel?

- Anti-lock brakes or traction control?

Cockpit Drill

- All doors closed (locking the doors prevents someone entering the vehicle to assault officers, but delays assistance in the event of an accident).

- Handbrake on.

- Seat adjusted (test the position – officers should comfortably be able to grip the top of the steering wheel with their back resting against the seat).

- Seat belt on (disregard those who say, 'I've lost too many prisoners wearing my seat belt!' – wear it).

- Mirrors adjusted to maximise rearward vision.

- Gears in neutral.

- Start engine.

- Check warning lights.

- Fuel level (do not leave a vehicle with less than half a tank full of fuel, ideally it should be at least three quarters full).

- Instrument check, indicators, lights, horn.

- Static brake test – there should be a good firm pressure. Sponginess may indicate air in the brake system.

- Check log book for any faults reported.

- Debris in vehicle?

Moving Brake Test

When travelling on a safe stretch of road conduct a moving brake test. Whilst driving at 30 mph in top gear check for other road users and, if safe, brake firmly down to 10 mph and then take second gear. The brake test should reveal a good firm braking action with no adverse effect on the steering. Any other effects, eg, spongy braking or the steering pulling to one side, must be investigated.

If officers cannot find a good stretch of road to perform the moving brake test then they should brake early for the first hazard, such as the first road intersection.

ROUTINE PATROL DRIVING

The Police Driver's Handbook Roadcraft was comprehensively revised in 1994. There can be no better publication on police driving skills than this new Roadcraft.

Accidents often occur when there is insufficient space to take avoiding action to prevent a collision. Every effort should go into concentrating on driving to anticipate hazards there by creating **time to react**. As speed increases drivers must concentrate harder as safety margins are reduced. The following elements are essential to safe patrol driving.

Driving Ability

Police officers need to take a realistic approach to their own driving ability. If officers are not trained to drive a vehicle at speed then they must drive at a speed they are comfortable with. Good drivers are those who know their own limitations and drive accordingly.

The Safety Position

Whatever the road conditions officers should position their patrol vehicle in the safest place on the road. By using observation skills they identify hazards, such as other road users, and allow adequate safety margins.

Observation Links

Good observation is a prerequisite of patrol driving. Officers must scan the road ahead, the periphery, and the mirrors. The extent of their vision is one determining factor in the safe use of speed. With good observation linked to an anticipation of what may occur officers should be able to stop within the distance they can see to be clear.

RESPONSE DRIVING

Response driving is a skilled area for drivers of emergency vehicles who attend incidents using speed with safety. **There is no substitute for sound driver training in response techniques**. The purpose of this section is to cover the justification for a 'response drive'.

Response driving will almost undoubtedly involve the contravention of traffic laws, such as the speed limit. Police drivers are exempt from certain traffic legislation if observance of the particular law would be 'likely to hinder the use of the vehicle for the purpose for which it is being used on that occasion'. Contravention of a solid white line system is not a legal exception. Police officers cannot therefore rely on a 'legal exemption' if they cross a solid white line whilst overtaking a moving vehicle.

Each situation must be considered objectively to see if legal exemptions were justified. If the situation changed en route the question of whether legal exemptions were still justified would need to be addressed. If an officer responds to a personal attack alarm at a bank and contravened traffic laws he or she may well be justified in claiming legal exemption. If the first patrol car arrives at the bank and declares that it is purely an alarm fault, it would be difficult for the officer still en route to the bank to justify contravening traffic laws.

When en route to an emergency assess the following:

Objective

One force's graded response criteria for immediate response is a follows:

I   There is danger to life.

I   Violence is being used or threatened.

I   A serious crime (violent crime/burglary) is in progress or is likely to occur.

I   A suspect for a serious crime is nearby.

I   There has been a road traffic accident involving personal injury to other road users.

I   A person who is especially vulnerable needs assistance.

This is a good guide as to what may constitute justification for a response drive.

Environment

I   Prevailing traffic conditions.

I   Distance to be travelled to the scene.

I   Justification for the use of legal exemptions, warning lights and sirens.

I   Approaching without sirens may improve chances of apprehending offender, but officers must drive slower than they would with lights and sirens as the public would expect a police car responding to an emergency to be using the emergency equipment.

Self

I   The suitability of the police vehicle and level of driver for the purpose.

When using beacons and sirens police officers should expect that other road users will do absolutely **anything**, from stopping dead, speeding up or moving into their path. Officers must drive defensively, that is expect the worst from other road users.

PURSUIT DRIVING

The deaths of criminals or innocent parties in police pursuits represent a tiny fraction of the overall death toll on the roads. However the adverse media coverage which police pursuit deaths attract is considerable.

A police officer's chance of being involved in an accident whilst engaged in a pursuit have been calculated at over a thousand times greater, mile for mile, than when engaged on routine patrol driving. Police pursuits therefore are not to be entered into lightly.

As with response driving, police pursuits should be conducted by trained officers in vehicles suitable for the purpose. If the pursuit is initiated by an untrained officer he or she must disengage from the pursuit when a trained officer takes over.

This section deals with the grounds for pursuing vehicles.

Objective

I How grave is the offence?

I Can the matter be dealt with at a later date?

Subject

I Is the subject known to officer?

I Is the subject a juvenile?

Environment

I What are the road, traffic and weather conditions?

Re-assess the pursuit when factors change, for example:

> 'At 4 pm on a weekday during school term the pursuit enters a densely populated built up area at high speed.'

> 'At 11 pm an unlit subject vehicle drives the wrong way down a busy dual carriageway.'

Where it appears that a pursuit would be futile or the danger to all involved cannot be justified **then disengage**. Two police pursuit vehicles is normally the maximum allowed in a pursuit. The caravaning of numerous unsuitable police vehicles behind the subject vehicle only adds to the danger.

Own Resources

I Consider the timely use of air support if available.

I Consider the deployment of stinger (hollow road spikes designed for a controlled deflation of a tyre) if available.

I A police dog handler is an invaluable asset should the occupants of the pursued vehicle run off.

Commentary

The observer in the first pursuit vehicle should take up a commentary. The commentary should be crisp and accurate. It should be borne in mind that the commentary may be recorded for evidential purposes, and it should include:

I Who you are – your callsign.

I Where you are.

I What is the subject vehicle? Description of vehicle and its occupants.

I What are the occupant(s) of the subject vehicle responsible for?

I Direction of travel and the name of each road the vehicle travels along, include speed and any traffic violations committed.

I The actions of the occupant(s) especially if they appear to be about to decamp, eg,

'Turning right, right into Dover Close.
It's a dead end.
Vehicle braking.
Doors opening.
Vehicle stopped three suspects out on foot towards the flats.'

I Give a result at the end:
Any injuries?
Any vehicles damaged?
Any arrests?
Any evidence to be recovered?
Any accidents to be recorded?

Cool Down

After a pursuit, due to the effects of adrenaline, officers may experience some disorientation. They may be excited, frightened, relieved, frustrated, angry.

It is important to recognise that these feelings exist and that to return to a normal emotional state requires a little time. It may be a good idea for officers to park up for a while or drive slowly back to their police stations for a beverage. Some forces, eg, the West Midlands Police, have a form to complete at the end of each pursuit. Completing this sort of form allows officers to concentrate on something else rather than reliving the pursuit they were just involved in. Just as drivers modify their speed when they leave the motorway for an A class road, so officers should make a conscious effort to adjust from pursuit driving to routine patrol driving.

If officers decided to discontinue a pursuit for safety reasons they may be criticised by their colleagues. It is better to err on the side of caution rather than continue with a dangerous pursuit.

SUMMARY

Taking care of the patrol fleet is an officer's responsibility as a professional. Officer safety depends upon the vehicles being roadworthy.

Defensive driving is a valuable skill which can save officers' lives both on and off duty.

Response and pursuit driving are specialised forms of driving which should only be undertaken by trained officers and only where the circumstances justify it.

Recommended Reading

Roadcraft, The Police Driver's Handbook, HMSO.

Chapter fifteen
CONCLUSION

Chapter fifteen

Conclusion

There is no magic key to reducing danger and therefore improve officer safety. If the reader is the type of person who starts a book by reading the last chapter, this statement may have come as a disappointment.

Everyone involved in officer safety needs to apply themselves to reduce the incidence of officers being killed or injured. The purpose of this chapter is to propose a system to improve officer safety.

OFFICER SAFETY SYSTEM

Officer safety is dynamic. New equipment and techniques are being introduced to counter new threats. Police officers need to keep revising their knowledge and skills to keep up with developments. How are you going to do that?

Every incident involving an officer being injured or killed is a story waiting to be told. Officers have suffered and little has been learned to prevent a recurrence. It is painful to review the actions of officers who have been injured or even killed. There are often lessons that can learned by investigating these incidents which may help other officers survive similar events. What system is there to draw conclusions from such incidents? When conclusions have been drawn from hard won experience how are these translated into recommendations and implemented?

One solution to all these questions is an Officer Safety System to be established in each police force. It is represented in the facing diagram.

The objective of the system is to improve the safety of operational police officers; it is a process of reducing the dangers they face.

Examples of inputs to this process are:

▌ Personnel.

▌ Training.

▌ Equipment.

▌ Procedures.

These inputs can all be affected. More officers can be input; new training methods can be used; better equipment can be bought; new procedures can be stated. (The means to change these inputs are labelled 'actuators'.)

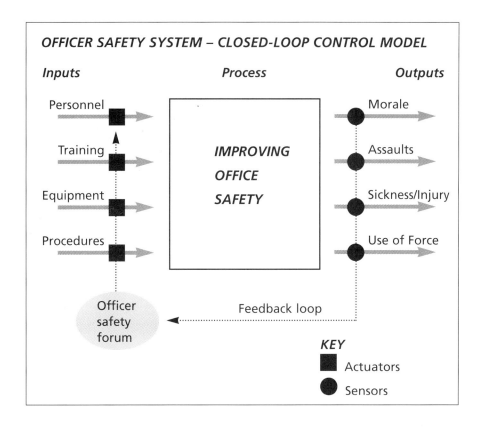

Just some examples of outputs which can be measured are:

I Morale.

I Assaults on police officers.

I Sickness and injury.

I Use of force.

All these outputs can all be measured by 'sensors'. A procedure which collects data on police assaults is a sensor. For these measurements to be meaningful the report formats must be standardised throughout the country.

The system has a process (improving officer safety) which has inputs (personnel, training, etc) and outputs (morale, assaults, etc). These outputs can be measured and the inputs can be modified.

Standards need to be set on the outputs. For example if 90% of incidents where handcuffing techniques were tried were successful on the streets, this might mean that the use of handcuffs is effective. However, if only 10% of handcuffings were successful then this needs to be analysed and improvements implemented. Where is the line drawn? Targets, standards, performance indicators, whatever name is given to them, establish a base line. If the output fails to achieve the standard it must be analysed.

It must be decided what is an acceptable standard or the system will be reacting to every minor failing in operational practice. As an example, it would be reasonable that the standard set for officers killed on duty would be zero. Every time an officer is killed the system will be activated and analyse the circumstances.

Once standards have been set to trigger the system, a forum needs to be assembled to compare the output with the goal of improving officer safety and affecting the inputs. The forum needs to have executive power to change the inputs.

If there is an unacceptable percentage of successful uses of batons this triggers the forum to analyse the problem. If the recommendation appears to be a new piece of equipment or a revised training method, the forum must have the power to buy equipment or change the training. The head of the forum must have the power (ie rank and budget) to get things done. Officers' lives are involved and the forum must not be simply a 'talking shop'.

The terms of reference for the officer safety forum must be fairly rigid. It must focus on the physical safety of operational officers. It would be too easy for the direction of the forum to drift into discussing expenses for officers on standby duty and things of that nature. The system must not allow the banner of 'officer safety' to be misused. It could become the excuse which some cynical people would use to satisfy their own agenda.

The forum must have credibility in the eyes of operational officers. Although it may be headed by an officer of ACPO rank and have Police Federation and training advisors, the majority of the members must be operational. Each division or area could nominate an operational officer to represent their views. It would be these liaison officers who would investigate incidents where officers have suffered injury and gather evidence related to officer safety. The officer safety forum would then decide on what lessons could be learned to communicate this information. A way must be found to avoid the discovery areas of improvement becoming yet another avenue which a desperate legal defence could use to attack the actions of police officers. It may be that report forms could be submitted by police officers anonymously.

Before policy decisions are taken affecting officer safety the forum should be consulted.

This system will provide detailed information on officer safety issues. If criticism is levelled at police officers' increasing readiness to use force this can be checked against the outputs from the officer safety system. This will counter criticism which is unfounded and based on anecdotal evidence.

As well as learning from officers' own experience, there is a wealth of information about officer safety out there. There are dozens of books written on officer safety topics as well as organisations with electronic mail to update officers on the latest developments. These books tend to come from America. Due to our common language and culture these sources of information are easily accessible by people in Britain.

There is much that British officers can learn from the experience of American police officers. Although most European police forces tend to be based on a military structure there would be merit in learning from them as well.

However policing in Britain is a unique experience, it is mainly unarmed for a start. There is scope to learn a great deal more about officer safety from our own experiences. This is why an Officer Safety System is so important.

Should each force adopt its own Officer Safety System the lessons learned and best practice must be shared. If each force was linked by an electronic network, such as Epicentre (Police Scientific Development Branch), then information could be passed instantaneously.

If some sort of systematic approach is not adopted police officers will not learn the lessons from their own hard won experiences. It is only with a system which senses performance and can respond appropriately that officer safety can be genuinely improved.

In the real world of policing it is unlikely that many forces would establish the system described above. Organisations do not usually surrender executive power and budgets; often there are other competing needs which are considered more important. The police service's greatest asset is human resources. What need is more important than reducing the risks to the operational police officer? Forces may not implement the system fully; instead the system could have an advisory role, rather than an executive one.

OFFICER SAFETY TRAINING

Officer safety training has been compared with a brick wall without mortar. Each brick represents a different training specialism, handcuffs, batons, firearms, tactical communications, self-defence, knife defence and riot control.

What is lacking is the 'mortar' to bind each specialism together to form a co-ordinated whole. The result is confusion for the operational officer, 'Do I call out the ARV? Or should I go in and use an empty handed technique or my handcuffs or my baton?'

Trainers should cross-train so they have a broad spectrum of officer safety knowledge.

All of these bricks should be officer safety training and be based on reality. Training should be done wearing normal operational equipment. The students should create the scenarios to be dealt with, based on their own experiences on the streets. If it does not work on the streets it should not be taught. Complex techniques involving intricate manoeuvres are for amusement as party tricks, not for operational use. In the past defensive tactics training appears to have been trainer-led, rather than what the operational officer actually wanted or used in practice. CCTV around the country is recording a large number of incidents where officers have had to arrest violent people. What techniques did the officers use in reality to effect the arrests? If the techniques which are actually used can be analysed the police service could incorporate them into training packages.

Human brains seem to have a capacity for remembering only a handful of items in the short-term. In psychology there is a term, 'The Magic Seven'; we tend to be able to remember about seven items. (This may be why registration plates are a maximum of seven characters long.) Why is it that police officers are expected to remember dozens of empty handed, baton and handcuff techniques? It has been proved that the more techniques police officers learn the slower their reaction time becomes, as they have to select mentally which technique they are going to use. There could be an argument for trainers to demonstrate a range of techniques and allowing the officers to choose which ones they want to become proficient in. After all it is going to be the officers who will have to rely on the techniques on the streets.

If there is a reduction in the number of physical techniques taught to officers this should not mean a reduction in the numbers of trainers. The writer hopes that this book demonstrates that there is scope for developmental training in officer safety which does not necessarily include the physical skills, such as assessing, communicating and reporting the use of force.

Traditionally self-defence techniques have been taught using one officer to one subject scenarios. Martial arts use this system so that individuals can be assessed for grading purposes. Operational encounters are rarely one-to-one. Often one officer has to cope with two or more subjects plus bystanders. There might also be one subject and multiple officers. Training needs to be based on reality. Police officers should learn how to cope with multiple assailants as well as how to work as a team with other officers, say on a takedown tactic. The use of video taping in dynamic training is a great aid and should be widely used. The successful completion of a total package of officer safety training should be recognised by the presentation of something worthwhile such as a search stick. This is a lightweight, touch sensitive tapered tube used for safe body and vehicle searching.

Many police officers have been killed encountering an assailant at close quarters armed with a firearm. Officers may be trained in knife defence, but what training have they received in immediate actions against a firearm threat? There are tactics to use when faced with a firearm, but training is needed. Body armour is not a complete solution; it only buys officers time after they have been shot once. There are innovative means to train officers in firearm encounters which use paint ball equipment. This area of training should be addressed before more officers are injured by the criminal use of firearms.

An essential part of street survival is physical conditioning. It must be accepted that fitness training will be done in officers' own time. There are ways to encourage officers to undertake a fitness programme. An annual Fitness Bounty could be paid to officers who reach a minimum fitness level. The bounty could be in the form of a voucher to the value of half an annual subscription to a local leisure facility. Police officers would still have to pay half the subscription themselves and maintain a standard of fitness. Having multi-gym facilities in police stations is not normally as attractive an option as visiting a local leisure centre. There are many imaginative ways the police service can and should encourage improvements in the fitness of their officers.

OFFICER SAFETY EQUIPMENT

The image of the police officer has changed so much that the police should concentrate on functionality not tradition. Police uniforms should be designed to reflect the real world of policing today. Traditionalists will obstruct changes to police uniform, but functionality must come first.

PERSONAL RESPONSIBILITY

There are many improvements which the organisation can make to improve officer safety. These improvements are worth nothing if officers have a complacent attitude towards their own safety.

If officers were to concentrate on the following areas their safety would be improved:

I Be aware of the circumstances in which you are most likely to be assaulted, eg, assailant profile, location, time of day, etc.

I Know the threat posed by firearms and edged weapons. Learn the immediate actions on encountering such a threat.

I Assess your fitness level. Set a realistic fitness target and undertake a regular fitness programme.

I Learn the basics of survival, ie, States of Survival Awareness, Reactionary Gap, Relative Positioning, Contact and Cover and Body Posture.

I Check your protective equipment regularly.

I Assess logically.

I Communicate effectively.

I Search safely.

I Arrest safely.

I Escort safely.

I Review your driving.

I Acquire training in first aid.

I Know how to justify your use of force in writing.

I Practice the physical skills of self-defence, baton and handcuffs.

It is essential to keep an open and enquiring mind. Police officers need to reflect on their performance and strive constantly to improve.

The motto of one training organisation is:

'Your survival begins and ends with you.'

This is very true, so train and equip yourself for the worst. Think tactically and survive!

APPENDIX

USE OF FORCE – ARRESTING OFFICER'S STATEMENT

This Appendix should be read in conjunction with Chapter Nine – The Use of Force. The comments in capitals highlight certain points, but would not actually appear in a statement.

'At 01.45 Hours on Sunday the 21st April 19XX I attended outside Wolfie's Night Club, Main Street, Anytown, where I saw a man who I know to be the defendant, Alan Jenkins.

(ATTENDANCE DETAIL) I was on solo uniformed patrol in a liveried police five door hatchback car.

I parked the patrol car at the front of the night club and started to walk towards the front door.

(INITIAL OBSERVATIONS OF THE DEFENDANT) The defendant was standing at the hot-dog stand about 10 metres away on my left.

As I walked towards the front door the defendant shouted at me, "All police are bastards!"

(GRAVITY OF THE OFFENCE, INFLUENCE OF ANGER AND ALCOHOL) At the front door of the night club I saw a male member of the door staff who I know to be, Phil Cameron, sitting down. His nose was profusely bleeding and the front of his shirt was covered in blood.

He said to me, "That guy over there by the hot-dog stand has just belted me because I wouldn't let him in. He's drunk." He pointed at the defendant.

(CAPABILITY OF THE DEFENDANT)The manager of the night club, Peter Green, said, "I saw it all officer. That man just punched Phil for no reason. It was completely unprovoked. Be careful he's quite a handful I've seen him in action before, he's into martial arts I think."

(THE "SUBJECT" IMPACT FACTORS CONSIDERED IN YOUR ASSESSMENT) The defendant was alleged to have committed a serious assault punishable by a term of imprisonment.

The defendant was known to me and I believed at the time that there was an arrest warrant in force for him.

From what the witnesses said I felt that the defendant had consumed alcohol and was aggressive.

The defendant was standing by the hot-dog stand. On the counter of the hot-dog stand were two knives within easy reach. One was a small serrated kitchen knife and the other was a larger bread knife.

He was wearing a loose fitting bomber type jacket which could easily have concealed other weapons.

There were a couple of men standing in the taxi queue a few metres away who were speaking to the defendant in a friendly manner. I took these two men to be friends of the defendant.

I would describe the defendant as a white male, 25 to 30 years of age, approximately 6'4" tall of a muscular build. From what I had been told I suspected that the defendant had a knowledge of combat skills, namely martial arts.

From my previous dealings with the defendant I knew that he has several previous convictions for assault, damage and drunkenness.

From what he shouted at me I assumed that he was in an argumentative, if not aggressive frame of mind.

(THE 'ENVIRONMENT' IMPACT FACTORS CONSIDERED IN YOUR ASSESSMENT) The area around the hot-dog stand was busy with people leaving the night-club, heading for the taxi rank and the take-away next door to the night club.

The take-away had a large queue of people spilling out onto the pavement in sight of the hot-dog stand.

From previous experience I knew that in the next couple of minutes a flood of people would leave the night club as it closed. It was important to effect the arrest without delay before the area became full of intoxicated people leaving the club who were likely to hamper my actions.

(THE 'OWN RESOURCES' IMPACT FACTORS CONSIDERED IN YOUR ASSESSMENT) I requested that the police personnel carrier and crew attend to assist me in arresting the defendant.

The defendant was at least four inches taller than me and had more skill combat sports than I do. I had been working since 2 pm the preceding day. It had been a busy shift and I was particularly tired having just recovered from a heavy cold. I was equipped with a pair of rigid handcuffs and a side handled baton.

(DESCRIPTION OF CONTROL EQUIPMENT)The rigid handcuffs are designed to control, rather than merely restrain, a subject by applying pressure to the wrist joint as I have been instructed on an approved training programme.

The side handled baton is a multi-purpose defensive instrument intended to protect the user and restrain subjects following an approved training programme.

(SUBJECT BEHAVIOUR) I saw the defendant start pointing his right index finger at the hot-dog stand owner. The defendant shouted at the man, "Now listen here mate. I gave you a soddin' twenty pound note so give me my change or I'll punching your friggin' lights out!"

(VERBAL COMMAND) I approached the defendant from behind and said, "Move away from the hot-dog stand."

(SUBJECT RESPONSE) The defendant turned around and leant against the hot-dog stand and folded his arms. He said, "You can frig off". I moved to his left hand side about two metres away.

(VERBAL COMMAND) Again I said, "Move away from the hot-dog stand."

(SUBJECT RESPONSE) The defendant turned to face me and started walking straight towards me.

(VERBAL COMMAND) I said, "Standstill".

(SUBJECT RESPONSE) The defendant continued to walk directly towards me.

(DRAWING BATON CONTROL METHOD) I stepped back and to my right, drawing my baton in a crossdraw into the basic position as I had been taught to do when threatened. The basic position is holding the baton horizontal with the strong hand (my right hand) on the short handle and the long extended portion running rearwards along the forearm.

(VERBAL COMMAND) Again I said, "Standstill! Now!"

(SUBJECT RESPONSE) This time the defendant stopped and said, "Allright what's all this bloody nonsense about then?"

(EVIDENCE OF DRUNKENNESS) The defendant's breath smelt strongly of alcohol. He rocked forwards and backwards on his feet as he stood facing me. His were reddened and watery. He was drunk.

(ASSESSMENT) He had now unfolded his arms and had his right hand behind his back. I felt that this was a threatening gesture as the defendant could well have a concealed weapon in the rear waistband area of his trousers.

(VERBAL COMMAND) I said, "Put both arms out to the side."

(SUBJECT RESPONSE) The defendant slowly raised both arms.

(VERBAL COMMAND) I said, "Lock out your elbows. Open your hands and spread your fingers."

(SUBJECT RESPONSE)The defendant slowly complied and said, "You're making a big mistake. Do you know who I am?" A man in the taxi queue who I do not know shouted, "Go on Jenksie, take the mouthy git!" The defendant stared at me and smiled.

(EVIDENCE OF ARREST) I replaced my baton and approached the defendant on his left side and said to him, "You are under arrest for assaulting a member of the door staff at Wolfie's night club," and I cautioned him to which he made no reply.

(ESCORT HOLD CONTROL METHOD) I took hold of the defendant's left arm in an escort hold. With my right hand I took hold of the defendant's upper left arm. With my left hand I took hold of the defendant's left wrist.

(VERBAL COMMAND) I said to him, "Over to the car". I gently pushed the defendant in the direction of the police car.

(SUBJECT RESPONSE) The defendant said, "If you think I'm going without a fight you can think again dickhead!"

(VERBAL COMMAND) I said to the defendant, "Over to the car".

(SUBJECT RESISTANCE) The defendant replied, "No way," I saw the defendant's right arm swing back and his hand formed a clenched fist. I felt him try to pull me with his left arm. His body began pivoting quickly round and I lost sight of right arm. I believed that I was about to be punched.

(EMPTY HAND CONTROL METHOD) I pushed the defendant away from me quickly to avoid being punched. He stumbled forwards and fell on his knees. I stepped back and drew my baton again into the basic position.

(SUBJECT BEHAVIOUR) The defendant got up and moved towards me. He had both hands raised in a boxer's stance. Both of his fists were clenched. He was staring at me and his teeth were bared.

(VERBAL COMMAND) When he was two metres away I shouted, "Get back!" at the defendant.

(SUBJECT BEHAVIOUR) The defendant kept on coming towards me jabbing the air with his left fist and exhaling sharply each time he threw a punch. Each punch was directed at my head.

(ASSESSMENT OF THREAT) From the training I have received I know that the head is a final target area. Any injury to a final target area tends to be of a permanent nature. A blow to the head can easily cause unconsciousness or even death. I felt threatened for my safety by the defendant's actions. I was scared.

(BATON SPIN CONTROL METHOD) When he was only a short distance from me I shouted, "Get back!" and performed a forward spin at full force with the baton intending to strike the defendant's upper left thigh.

A forward spin is performed by holding the short handle in the strong hand and allowing the long extended portion to spin horizontally as the strong hand moves in front of the body to the weak side. The thigh area is a primary target area. A blow struck to a primary target area will result in a minimal level of trauma. Any injury to a primary target area tends to be temporary. The objective of a strike to a primary target area is to decentralise the subject, that is to knock him off balance and thereby reduce his capability of assaulting me.

The baton missed and the defendant kept on coming towards me. I performed a reverse spin at full force with the baton again

aiming to strike the defendant's thigh. The long extended portion of the baton struck the defendant's upper right thigh.

The defendant stumbled then fell forwards and lay spread eagled on the pavement. A reverse spin is a horizontal spin from the weak side to the strong side.

(SUBJECT RESISTANCE) I knelt on the left hand side of the defendant who was starting to get up.

(VERBAL COMMAND) I shouted, "Stay down!"

(SUBJECT RESISTANCE) The defendant continued to try and get up.

(EMPTY HAND CONTROL METHOD) I placed my right knee on his upper left arm to restrain him by pinning it to the ground. I replaced my baton and drew my rigid handcuffs. With the bottom cuff I handcuffed the defendant's left wrist from the little finger side of the wrist.

(SUBJECT RESISTANCE) The defendant said, "Get the frig off me!" and started to try and get up.

(HANDCUFF CONTROL METHOD) I again shouted, "Stay down!" but the defendant continued to struggle so I took control of his left wrist and tightened the bottom cuff with my right hand. With my left hand I applied pressure on the wrist as I have been trained to do and said, "Put your hand behind your back."

(SUBJECT COMPLIANCE) The defendant shouted, "Bastard!" and put right hand behind his back.

(HANDCUFFING DETAIL) I released the pressure on the wrist and took hold of the defendant's right hand. I then handcuffed both of the defendant's hands together, back to back. I searched the rear waistband area of the defendant's trousers. I then checked the handcuffs for tightness before double locking them to prevent the single bars tightening around the defendant's wrists.

A liveried police personnel carrier arrived and Constables 8639 Netherton and 7524 Rowland assisted me.

(VERBAL COMMAND AND TEAM TACTIC CONTROL METHOD) I said to the defendant, "We're going to help you up now. Just get your knees up towards your stomach." As the defendant complied Constable Netherton and I supported the defendant's shoulder joints from underneath. When the defendant got onto his feet we walked him to the personnel carrier.

(TRANSPORT DETAIL AND SUBJECT'S DEMEANOUR) We assisted the defendant into the secure cage at the rear of the personnel carrier and sat him on the bench seat. The defendant shouted, "You ain't seen nothing yet. I'll swing for you when you take these 'cuffs off." When we closed the cage door the defendant started kicking it with both feet.

I followed the personnel carrier into the custody parking area of Police Station, Higher New Road, Anytown, which is less than a mile from Wolfie's night club. Constables Netherton, Rowland and I assisted the defendant out of the cage and walked him into the holding cell. The defendant kept repeating, "I'll take all three of you. You bastards!"

I explained the grounds for the arrest to the custody officer, Sergeant 9786 Wilson. The custody officer authorised the defendant's detention and instructed us to take the defendant directly to cell number five.

(TEAM TACTIC CONTROL METHOD) We escorted the defendant slowly down the cell corridor. We entered cell number five. I held the defendant's head whilst Constables Netherton and Rowland each held the defendant's shoulders. The cell was stripped of any loose objects by the gaoler, Constable 5887 Brown, who then stood by the door.

I said to the defendant, "We're going to put you face down on the floor. Go down onto your knees." The defendant dropped down onto his knees.

I turned the defendant's head to the right to prevent injury and said, "Just lower yourself onto your front."

The defendant complied and lay on his front with his head closest to the cell door. I searched the defendant thoroughly and placed all his property in a plastic bag which was later recorded on his custody record.

The other officers had applied wrist restraints to both of the defendant's hands and removed the handcuffs. The defendant's wrists were restrained by application of pressure to the backs of the hands. I took hold of both wrists and the other officers left the cell. I sprang backwards and left the cell.

(INJURY DETAIL) The defendant had reddening on both wrists where the rigid handcuffs were applied. There were no other visible injuries on the defendant.'

GLOSSARY

AFO	Authorised Firearms Officer
ARV	Armed Response Vehicle
CCTV	Closed Circuit Television
Control Room	Also Known as Radio Room or Information Room
CPTU	Central Planning and Training Unit
FSU	Firearm Support Unit
PACE	The Police and Criminal Evidence Act 1984
PNC	Police National Computer *(national database of criminals, vehicles, etc.)*
PSU	Police Support Unit *(police officers trained in public order tactics)*
RTA	Road Traffic Accident
NVC	Non-Verbal Communication

BIBLIOGRAPHY

ACPO (1992), *Staying Alive – Firearms Incidents*, Central Planning and Training Unit, Harrogate.

ACPO (1995), *Self Defence Manual*, Unpublished.

Adams, RJ, McTernan, TM and Remsberg, C, *Street Survival – Tactics for Armed Encounters*, Calibre Press, Northbrook Illinois.

Alpert, GP and Dunham, RG (1990), *Controlling Responses to Emergency Situations*.

Amaral, M (1995), *Officer Safety*, Griffin, San Jose, California.

Ashley, SD (1994), *Pursuit Management – Implementing a Control Continuum*, Law & Order.

Bailey, RJ (1992), *The Arguments For, and Against, the Double Crewing of Police Patrol Cars*, Unpublished.

Baratta, R (1993), *Fear, Law & Order*.

Beckley, A (1994), *Personal Liability of Police Officers*, Home Office.

Black, J (1994), *Mindstore*, Thorsons, London.

Boatman, P (1993), *Stay Alert. Stay Alive*, Police.

Boatman, P (1994), *Less Strikes, More Control*, Police.

Boatman, P (1994), *Too Hot to Handle*, Police.

Boatman, P (1994), *Words of Wisdom*, Police.

Boatman, P (1995), *Protect Yourself*, Police.

Boatman, P, *Tactical Communications*, Unpublished.

Brown, B (1994), *Assaults on Police Officers*, Home Office.

Burden, OP (1995), *The Baddies in Blue*, Police.

Cansdale, D, *Protecting Police on the Streets*, Policing Today.

Casey, C (1992), *A Handle on Violence*, Police Review.

Cheshire Constabulary, *Police Pursuit Codes of Practice*, Unpublished.

Clarke, M (1993), *Not so wild up west*, Police Review.

Chorlton, P (1995), *Staying Fit at Work*, Health Education Authority, London

Conlin, T (1996), *Verbal Judo – Teaching modern peace warriors the power of words*, Police Marksman

Coyne, P (1994), *Roadcraft – The Police Driver's Handbook*, HMSO

Crotty, JM (1995), *Mental Preparation – The First Tactic for Survival*, Law & Order.

Davison, J (1995), *The Good Practice Guide to Officer Safety*, Metropolitan Police Service.

Demetriou, G (1992), *The Cutting Edge of Edged Weapons Defence*, ASLET Journal.

Dunston, M (1995), *Spontaneous Knife Defence: A Training Perspective*, The Police Marksman.

Edwards, C (1989), *The Art of Calming*, Police Review.

Edwards, C (1995), *"Another Bloody Domestic"*, Police Review.

Eggar, R (1993), *The Royal Marines Total Fitness*, Vermilion, London.

FBI, *Tactical Emergency Vehicle Operations Centre – New Agent Manual*, Unpublished.

Fensterheim, H, and Baer, J (1975), *Don't Say Yes When You Want To Say No*, Warner Books, London.

Finn, M (1990), *The Cuff – As Strong as its Weakest Link*, Police Review.

Fraser, S (1994), *Legal Move*, Police Review.

Frisby, D (1994), *Two Force Continuum Models*, ASLET Journal.

Gibbons, S (1994), *Handle with Care*, Police Review.

Gibbons, S (1995), *The Sharp End*, Police Review.

Graham, V (1995), *Oceans Apart*, Police Review.

Graham, V (1995), *Let's Get Physical*, Police Review.

Graham, V (1996), *Tortured Minds*, Police Review.

Graham, V (1996), *Protective Streak*, Police Review.

Grassi, R (1995), *Officer Survival Workshop*, Law & Order.

Greville, M (1994), *Keep Your Edge*, Police Review.

Harris, RC, *Basic Groundfighting Survival Skills*, Unpublished.

Haslam, D (1994), *Not Another Guide to Stress in General Practice*, Medical Action Communications Ltd.

Hertig, CA (1993), *Officer Survival Training for the 90s*, ASLET Journal.

Hetherington, A (1994), *Human Resource Management in Times of Stress*, De Montfort University, Leicester.

HMIC (1995), *Facing Violence*, Home Office.

Hoffman, R and Collingwood, TR (1995), *Fit for Duty*, Human Kinetics, Illinois.

Howe, S (1994), *Safety Links*, Police Review.

Howe, S (1994), *Stop Watch*, Police Review.

Howe, S (1994), *The Search. A Survival Guide*, Police Review.

Howe, S (1995), *Safe Investment*, Police Review.

Howe, S (1995), *Armour Not Arms*, Police Review.

Johnson, SH, and Kutha, K (1993), *"Why Should I Be Physically Fit?"*, Law & Order.

Kissane, S (1992), *The Quik–Kuf Solution*, Police Review.

Kock, E, Kemp, T., and Rix, B. (1993), *Assessing the Expandable Side-Handled Baton*, Home Office.

Laux, M (1994), *An Investigation into Police Vehicle Accidents in the Hampshire Constabulary*, Unpublished.

Laux, M (1994), *Baton-Age*, Police Review.

Laux, M (1994), *Evaluation of the Extendable Batons*, Hampshire Constabulary.

Lawrence, G, *Police Reactive Defence System*, Unpublished.

Lawrence, G, *Police Self Defence and Restraint Techniques*, Unpublished.

Lesce, T (1995), *Multi–Agency Survival Training*, Law & Order.

Lindell, JW and Smith, TE (1990), *Use of the Cas–16 and Cas–21 Expandable Police Batons*, Fitzwilliam, New Hampshire.

Lindenfield, G (1986), *Assert Yourself*, Thorsons, London.

Lindenfield, G (1993), *Managing Anger*, Thorsons, London.

Lindsey, B (1993), *Mental Preparation for Officer Survival*, ASLET Journal.

Lindsey, B (1994), *Managing the Aggressor's Behaviour*, ASLET Journal.

Lopez, CH (1994), *The Will to Survive*, Law & Order.

Los Angeles Police Department, *Training Bulletins* (Various).

Lycholat, T (1990), *The Complete Book of Stretching*, The Crowood Press, Marlborough.

MacHovec, F (1993), *Talktactics – Communications Skills for Security Officers*, Unpublished.

McDonald, AJ (1995), *Chasing Disaster*, The Police Marksman.

McLelland, and Gresty, B (1988), *Schooling for the Streets*, Police Review.

Moxey, M, and McKenzie, I, *Assaults on Police*, Policing.

Noaks, L, Christopher, S, and Levi, M, *Why Police are Assaulted*, Policing.

Nowicki, E (1993), *Total Survival*, Performance Dimensions Publishing, Powers Lake, Wisconscin.

North Wales Police, *The Police Baton and Reasonable Force*, Unpublished.

Okoszko, LR (1994), *Edged Weapons Defensive Training – Combating a Growing Problem*, Law & Order.

Ouellette, R (1993), *Management of Aggressive Behaviour*, Performance Dimensions Publishing, Powers Lake, Wisconsin

Pence, K (1992), *Dynamic Control Simulation Basic Level*, Confrontation Training Specialists, Nashville Tennessee.

Pence, K (1992), *Coming Along Quietly*, Police Review.

Pettit, MJ (1993), *PSDB Ballistic Body Armour Standard*, Home Office.

Philips, S, and Cochrane, R (1991), *Assaults Against the Police*, School of Psychology, University of Birmingham.

Police Marksman Association (1994), *The Best of the Police Marksman 1976–1994*, Montgomery, Alabama.

Potter, K (1995), *Ahead of the Chase*, Police Review.

Pike, H (1994), *The ASPs Bite*, Police Review.

Piper, S (1996), *Hit or Mist*, Police Review.

Purdy, G (1995), *Breaking Point*, Police Review.

Ramsey, DA (1993), *Quik–Kuf Training Manual*, Quik–Kuf Systems Inc.

Remsberg, C (1986), *The Tactical Edge – Surviving High Risk Patrol*, Calibre Press, Northbrook, Illinois.

Remsberg, C (1995), *Tactics for Criminal Patrol*, Calibre Press, Northbrook, Illinois.

Richards, M (1991), *Life at the Sharp End*, Police Review.

Roach, L (1995), *Street Wise*, Police Review.

Roach, L (1995), *Sound on Safety*, Police Review.

Roach, L (1995), *Being Prepared*, Police Review.

Roach, L (1995), *Safety First*, Police Review.

Siddle, B (1988), *Pressure Point Control Tactics*, PPCT Management Systems Inc., Millstadt, Illinois.

Siddle, B (1994), *Survival Stress Reaction*, The Police Marksman.

Sheehan, K (1994), *Image Projection – Female Officer appearance impacts perceived effectiveness*, Law & Order.

St John Ambulance (1992), *First Aid Manual*, Dorling Kindersley, London.

Starrett, RR (1981), *The PR–24 Police Baton*, Monadnock Lifetime Products, Fitzwilliam, New Hampshire.

Studt, DA (1995), *Controlling the Subject*, Law & Order.

Swanton, B, and Walker, J. (1989), *Police Employee Health*, Australian Institute of Criminology.

Tanguay N (1991), *Police Officer's Response Guide to Crimes/Incidents in Progress*, Tanguay Publications, Wethersfield, Conneticut.

Tan, J, Hicks, D, and Parker, G (1991), *Stab Resistant Vests*, Home Office.

Thompson, G J, and Jenkins, J B (1993), *Verbal Judo – The Gentle Art of Persuasion*, Quill, New York.

Truncale, J, and Smith, TE (1994), *Monadnock Defensive Tactics System*, Monadnock PR–24 Training Council, Inc, Fitzwilliam, New Hampshire.

Truncale, J (1995), *Officer Survival: Defence Against Sudden Knife Attacks*, Law & Order.

Waddington, PAJ (1993), *Calling the Police*, Avebury, Aldershot.

Waddington, PAJ (1995), *Body Guards*, Police Review.

Watney, J (1987), *The Royal Marines Commandos Fitness & Survival Skills*, Hippocrene Books, New York.

Williams, GT (1993), *A Safer Technique for Uncuffing a Prisoner*, Police Marksman.

Williams, GT (1996), *Angles and capabilities – Tactics usefully defined*, Police Marksman

Wilson, C (1993), *Police-Citizen Interactions*, National Police Research Unit, Australia.

Wilson, C, Gross, P, and Beck, K (1994), *Managing the Risk of Patrol*, National Police Research Unit, Australia.

Wilson, P (1994), *Response Training Course*, Unpublished.

Young, DW, *Defensive Tactics Development Course*, Unpublished.

Zulawski, DE, and Wicklander, DE (1995), *Field Interviewing*, Law & Order